Zero to Python

A Beginner's Coding Pathway

DABBEERU PRIYANKA

PENTA ANJANEYULU

YENNI MANASWINI

Made with ❤on the Notion Press Platform

www.notionpress.com

Contents

To update the Table of Contents, please right-click the field and choose'Update Field' and 'Update Entire Table.' When you update the Contents field, the fonts would automatically change to the default 'Calibri' setting given by Word. You can manually select the text and change the font to 'Gandhi serif.' Please delete these instructions once you update the Table of Contents. For more details, please go through the Reference Guide.

Foreword

In today's digital age, coding has become a crucial skill, unlocking countless opportunities across various fields. Yet, for many, the world of programming remains daunting, filled with complex jargon and seemingly insurmountable challenges. That's where *Zero to Python: A Beginner's Coding Pathway* comes in—a book designed to break down those barriers and make coding accessible to everyone.

Python, with its simplicity and versatility, is the ideal language for beginners. This book takes you on a journey from knowing nothing about programming to confidently writing and understanding Python code. What makes this journey unique is the clear, thoughtful approach taken by the author, Dabbeeru Priyanka. With years of experience teaching and working with Python, Priyanka has crafted a guide that is not just informative but also engaging and approachable.

Whether you're looking to start a new career, develop a hobby, or simply understand the technology that powers the world around you, this book provides the perfect starting point. Through practical examples and hands-on exercises, you'll find yourself gaining skills and confidence as you progress through each chapter.

As you turn the pages, you'll see that coding isn't as intimidating as it might seem. In fact, it can be enjoyable, rewarding, and even fun. By the end of this book, you'll have laid a strong foundation in Python, ready to take on more advanced challenges or apply your newfound knowledge in creative ways.

I encourage you to embrace this opportunity, dive in with curiosity, and let *Zero to Python: A Beginner's Coding Pathway* be your guide into the exciting world of programming.

Happy coding!

Dabbeeru Priyanka

Asst. Professor, CSE Department

Preface

The world is becoming increasingly digital, and the ability to code has transformed from a specialized skill into a powerful tool that can open countless doors. Yet, many people still find themselves overwhelmed by the idea of learning programming, unsure of where to begin. I wrote *Zero to Python: A Beginner's Coding Pathway* to address this very challenge—to provide a clear, accessible guide that anyone can follow, regardless of their prior experience.

Python was the natural choice for this book because of its simplicity, readability, and wide range of applications. It's a language that welcomes beginners with open arms, making it possible to start writing useful programs quickly. Throughout this book, you'll learn the fundamental concepts of Python programming in a way that's easy to understand and apply.

My goal is to make this journey enjoyable and rewarding. Each chapter is designed to build your confidence, gradually introducing new concepts and reinforcing your learning with practical examples. By the end of this book, you'll not only have a solid grasp of Python basics, but also the skills to continue exploring and creating with this versatile language.

Whether you're looking to change careers, pursue a personal project, or simply enhance your problem-solving abilities, *Zero to Python* is your pathway to success. I hope this book inspires you to keep learning, keep experimenting, and most importantly, keep coding.

Thank you for choosing to start your programming journey with me. I'm excited to see where Python will take you!

Sincerely,
Dabbeeru Priyanka

Acknowledgments

Writing this book has been a rewarding journey, and it wouldn't have been possible without the support and encouragement of many individuals. A special thanks to my students and readers, whose enthusiasm for learning and curiosity have driven me to create a resource that is both accessible and comprehensive. Your questions and challenges have been invaluable in refining my approach to teaching Python.

This endeavor was initiated by the department to inspire students to engage in research and publish their findings, while carefully considering important aspects such as plagiarism, ethical standards, peer review, formatting, data integrity, and disclosure.

I wish to express my heartfelt thanks to our esteemed Director, Prof. V. V. Nageswara Rao, whose unwavering support has been instrumental throughout this journey. Additionally, I extend my deepest gratitude to our Principal, Dr. A.S. Srinivasa Rao, whose guidance was indispensable during the course of this work.

I also wish to express my sincere thanks to Dr. Ch. Ramesh, Professor & Dean (IQAC), Dr. U.D. Prasan, Professor & Dean (D & P), and Dr. Yegireddi Ramesh, Professor & HOD, for their continuous encouragement and support. Their contributions have been pivotal in making this publication possible.

The creation of this book would not have been possible without the unwavering support of our Dr. D. Sreeramulu, Dean (R&D) & Prof, who provided invaluable guidance and encouragement throughout the research process. While the responsibility for the content and adherence to copyright guidelines lies with the students.

Lastly, I wish to express my profound gratitude to our College Management for providing the necessary infrastructure and facilities during the course of this project. Their support has been a cornerstone in the successful completion of this publication. And I would like to acknowledge the open-source community and the creators of Python, whose dedication and contributions have made this powerful language available to everyone.

To all of you, thank you for being a part of this journey with me. I hope this book serves as a valuable tool for all who embark on their own programming path.

Prologue/Introduction

Welcome to *Zero to Python: A Beginner's Coding Pathway*, your gateway into the world of programming. Whether you're a complete novice or someone with a bit of experience looking to strengthen your skills, this book is designed to guide you through the essentials of Python in a way that is both clear and engaging.

Why Python? Among the many programming languages available today, Python stands out for its simplicity and versatility. It's a language that reads almost like English, making it approachable for beginners, yet powerful enough to be used by professionals in fields ranging from web development to artificial intelligence. Python's community is vast and supportive, which means you'll never be alone on your learning journey.

This book is structured to take you step by step from the very basics of Python to a level where you can confidently tackle real-world projects. You'll start by learning how to set up your programming environment and write your first lines of code. As you progress, you'll explore key programming concepts, such as variables, loops, functions, and more, all within the context of Python. By the end of this book, you'll have a solid foundation that will allow you to continue exploring Python or dive into more advanced topics.

But this book is more than just a collection of programming exercises. It's about fostering a mindset of curiosity, problem-solving, and creativity. As you work through the examples and challenges, you'll not only learn to code but also how to think like a programmer—breaking down problems, testing solutions, and iterating on your work until you find the best approach.

Learning to program is a journey, and every journey starts with a single step. By picking up this book, you've already taken that step. I'm excited to accompany you on this path, and I'm confident that by the end of *Zero to Python*, you'll be ready to take on the coding challenges that await you.

1. Introduction to Python

Introduction to Python

1. History:

Python was developed by Guido van Rossum, a Dutch programmer, while working at the Centrum Wiskunde & Informatica (CWI) in the Netherlands. During December 1989, around Christmas, Guido sought a hobby project and began working on a new interpreter for a programming language, which he later named Python, inspired by the TV show "Monty Python's Flying Circus." The first version (0.9.0) was released in February 1991.

Python 1.0, released in 1994, introduced features like lambda, map, filter, and reduce. Python 2.0 brought list comprehensions and a garbage collection system. On December 3, 2008, Python 3.0, also known as "Py3K," was released to address fundamental flaws in the language. Python, being open-source, became popular in the 2010s, finding applications in data analysis, processing, web development, and more. By 2015, it consistently ranked among the top 5 programming languages in industry surveys. Python's flexibility and support across multiple platforms have strengthened its position in various domains. While version 2.7, released in July 2010, marked the end of enhancements, support continued until 2020. Python 3, designed without backward compatibility, is better suited for modern needs like AI and machine learning.

1.1 Why the Name Python?

Guido van Rossum aimed for a unique, short, and slightly mysterious name. He chose "Python" after the British comedy series "Monty Python's Flying Circus" to reflect these qualities.

Python Version	Released Date
Python 1.0	Jan-94
Python 1.5	December 31, 1997
Python 1.6	September 5, 2000
Python 2.0	October 16, 2000
Python 2.1	April 17, 2001
Python 2.2	December 21, 2001
Python 2.3	July 29, 2003
Python 2.4	November 30, 2004
Python 2.5	September 19, 2006

Python 2.6	October 1, 2008
Python 2.7	July 3, 2010
Python 3.0	December 3, 2008
Python 3.1	June 27, 2009
Python 3.2	February 20, 2011
Python 3.3	September 29, 2012
Python 3.4	March 16, 2014
Python 3.5	September 13, 2015
Python 3.6	December 23, 2016
Python 3.7	June 27, 2018
Python 3.8	October 14, 2019

Python's versatility has made it applicable across various technical fields, including Machine Learning, Artificial Intelligence, Web Development, Mobile Applications, Desktop Applications, and Scientific Calculations.

1.2 Python Applications:

Python's general-purpose nature allows it to be used in nearly every domain of software development.

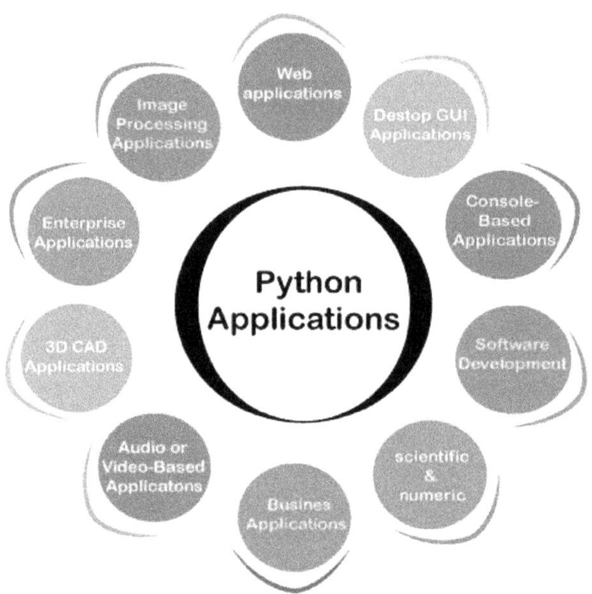

- **Web Applications:** Python is widely used for web application development, offering libraries to manage internet protocols like HTML, XML, and email processing. For instance, the Django web framework, built with Python, powers Instagram.
- **Desktop GUI Applications:** Python supports the development of graphical user interfaces (GUIs) using the Tk GUI library, enabling the creation of user-friendly desktop applications.
- **Console-based Applications:** Python excels in creating command-line or shell-based applications, with many free libraries and modules available for building command-line tools.
- **Software Development:** Python plays a key role in software development, serving as a support language for tasks like build control, management, and testing.
- **Scientific and Numeric Applications:** In the era of Artificial Intelligence, Python is the go-to language for AI and Machine Learning, thanks to its rich ecosystem of scientific and mathematical libraries like NumPy, Pandas, SciPy, and Scikit-learn. These libraries simplify complex calculations and data manipulations.
- **Business Applications:** Python is also employed in business applications, such as e-commerce and ERP systems, due to its scalability and robustness.
- **Audio or Video-based Applications:** Python is suitable for developing multimedia applications. Some well-known Python-based multimedia applications include TimPlayer and cplay. Libraries such as GStreamer and Pyglet support multimedia functionalities.
- **3D CAD Applications:** Python can be utilized to create 3D CAD (Computer-Aided Design) applications, which are essential in engineering design. Libraries like Fandango, AnyCAD, and RCAM facilitate the development of 3D representations of system components.
- **Enterprise Applications:** Python is widely used to develop enterprise-level applications that cater to organizational needs. For example, Odoo is an all-in-one Python-based suite offering a variety of business applications, and the Tryton platform is another Python-based framework for enterprise applications.
- **Image Processing Applications:** Python offers numerous libraries for image processing, enabling users to manipulate images according to their requirements. Some popular image processing libraries include OpenCV and SimpleITK.

2. Python Features:

Python provides many useful features which make it popular and valuable from the other programming languages. It supports object-oriented programming, procedural programming approaches and provides dynamic memory allocation. We have listed below a few essential features.

i) Easy to Learn and Use:

Python is very easy to learn the language as compared to other languages like C, C#, Javascript, Java, etc.. Its syntax is straightforward and much the same as the English language. There is no use of the semicolon or curly-bracket, the indentation defines the code block. It is the recommended programming language for beginners.

ii) Expressive Language:

Python can perform complex tasks using a few lines of code. A simple example, the hello world program you simply type print("Hello World"). It will take only one line to execute, while Java or C takes multiple lines.

iii) Interpreted Language:

Python is an interpreted language; it means the Python program is executed one line at a time. like other languages C, C++, Java, etc. there is no need to compile python code this makes it easier to debug our code. The source code of python is converted into an immediate form called bytecode.

iv) Python is Portable language:

Python language is also a portable language. For example, if we have python code for windows and if we want to run this code on other platforms such as Linux, Unix, and Mac then we do not need to change it, we can run this code on any platform.

v) Free and Open Source:

Python is freely available for everyone. It is freely available on its official website www.python.org. Anyone can contribute to the Python community. The open-source means, "Anyone can download its source code without paying any penny". Since it is open-source, this means that source code is also available to the public. So you can download it as, use it as well as share it.

vi) Object-Oriented Language:

Python supports object-oriented language and concepts of classes and objects come into existence. It supports inheritance, polymorphism, and encapsulation, etc. The object-oriented procedure helps to programmer to write reusable code and develop applications in less code.

vii) Extensible:

It implies that other languages such as C/C++ can be used to compile the code and thus it can be used further in our Python code. It converts the program into byte code, and any platform can use that byte code.

viii) Large Standard Library:

Python has a large standard library which provides a rich set of module and functions so you do not have to write your own code for every single thing.

It's libraries can be used in various fields such as machine learning, web developer, and also for the scripting. There are various machine learning libraries, such as Tensor flow, Pandas, Numpy, Keras, and Pytorch, etc. Django, flask, pyramids are the popular framework for Python web development.

ix) GUI Programming Support:

Graphical User interfaces can be made using a module such as PyQt5, PyQt4, wxPython, or Tk in python.

x) Integrated:

It can be easily integrated with languages like C, C++, and JAVA, etc. Python runs code line by line like C,C++ Java. It makes easy to debug the code.

xi) Embeddable:

The code of the other programming language can use in the Python source code. We can use Python source code in another programming language as well. It can embed other language into our code.

xii) Dynamic Memory Allocation:

In Python, we don't need to specify the data-type of the variable. When we assign some value to the variable, it automatically allocates the memory to the variable at run time. Suppose we are assigned integer value 15 to x, then we don't need to write int x = 15. Just write x = 15.

3. How to Install and Run Python on Windows:

Installing and running Python on your personal computer is no difficult task. It involves just a few simple steps:

Step 1: Gotothepythonwebsite**www.python.org**andclickonthe'Download'menuchoice.

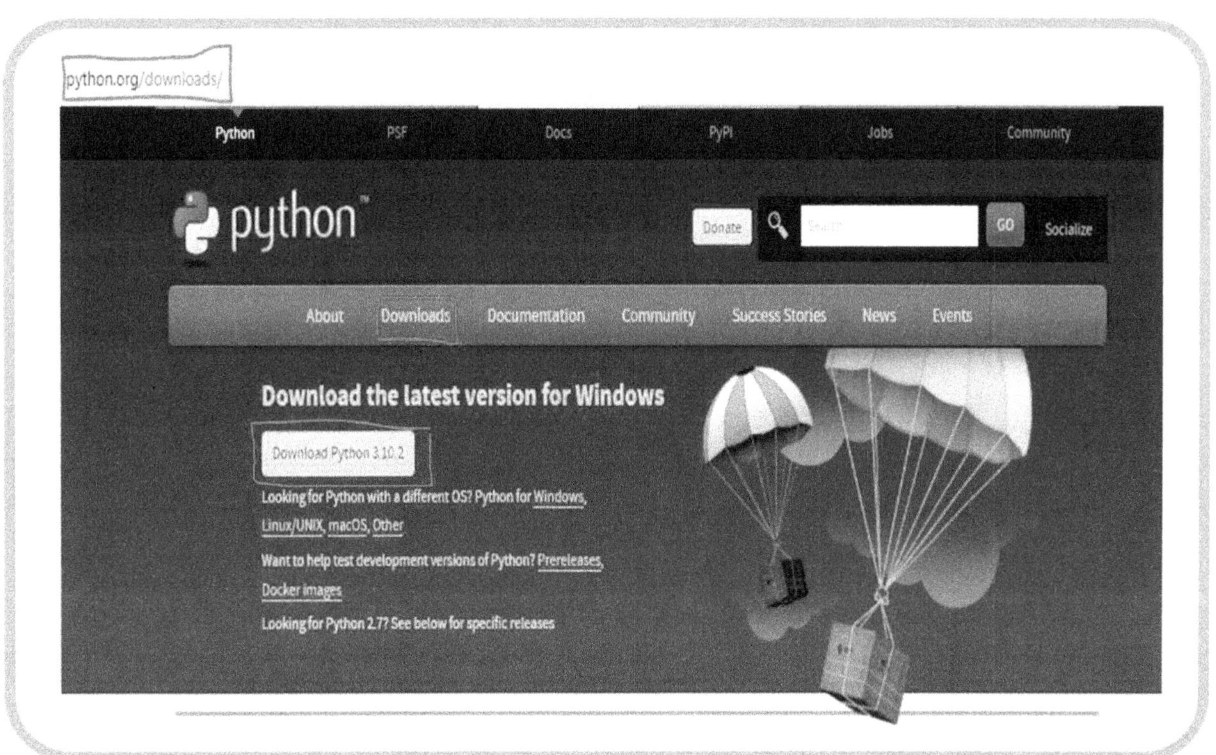

Step 2: Once the download is complete, run the .exe for install Python. Now click on Install Now.

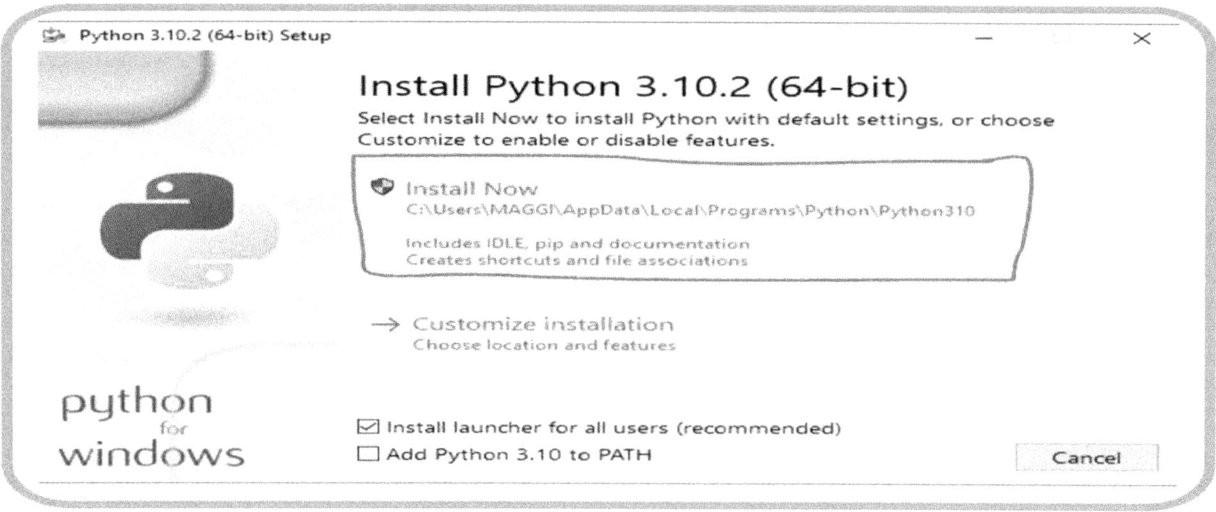

Step 3: You can see Python installing at this point.

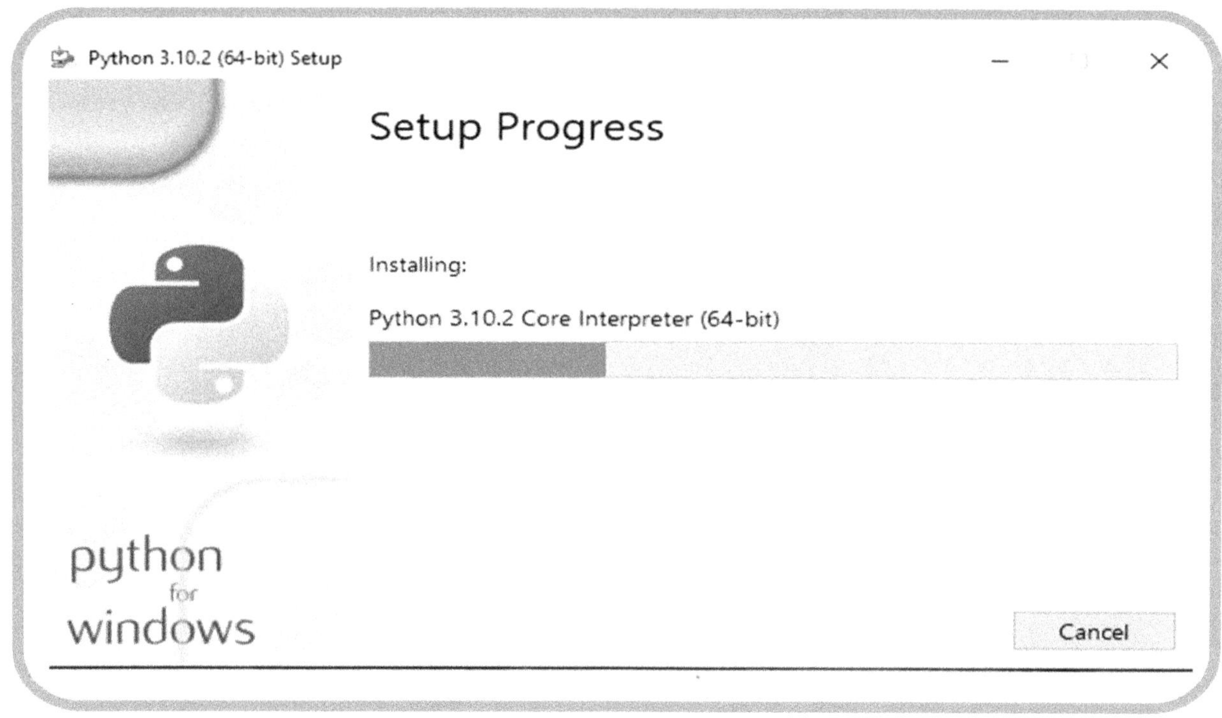

Step 4: When it finishes, you can see a screen that says the Setup was successful. Now click on "Close".

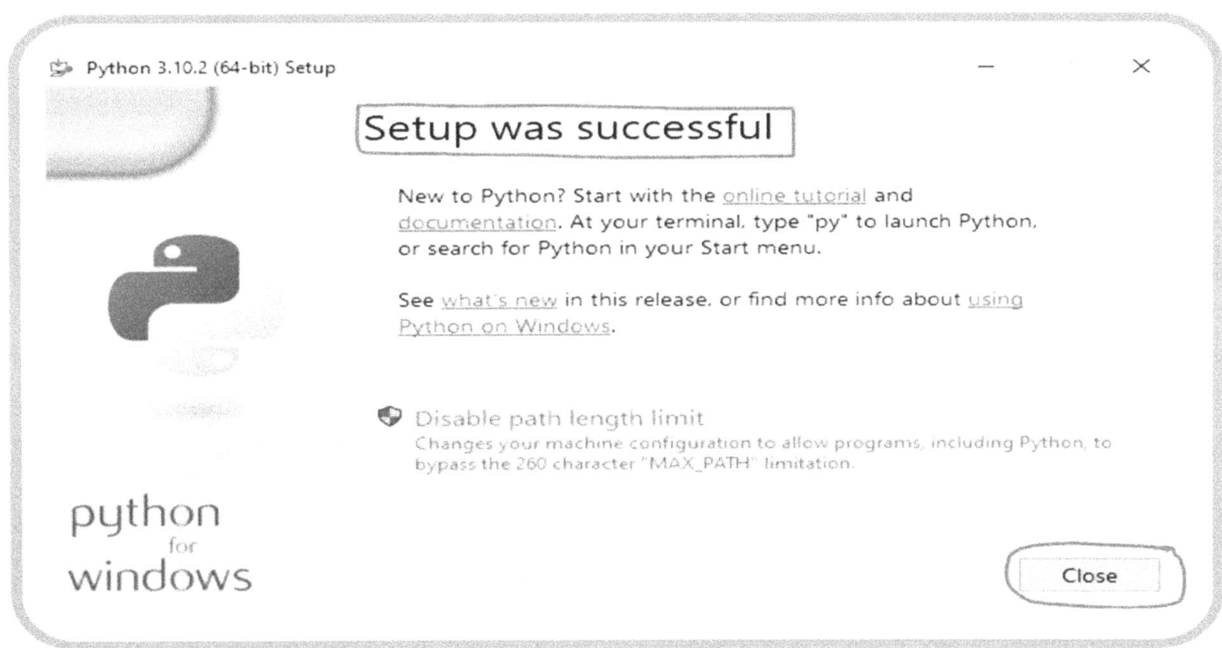

After installed, you should now have a Python menu choice. Start the program by choosing IDLE (Python GUI)

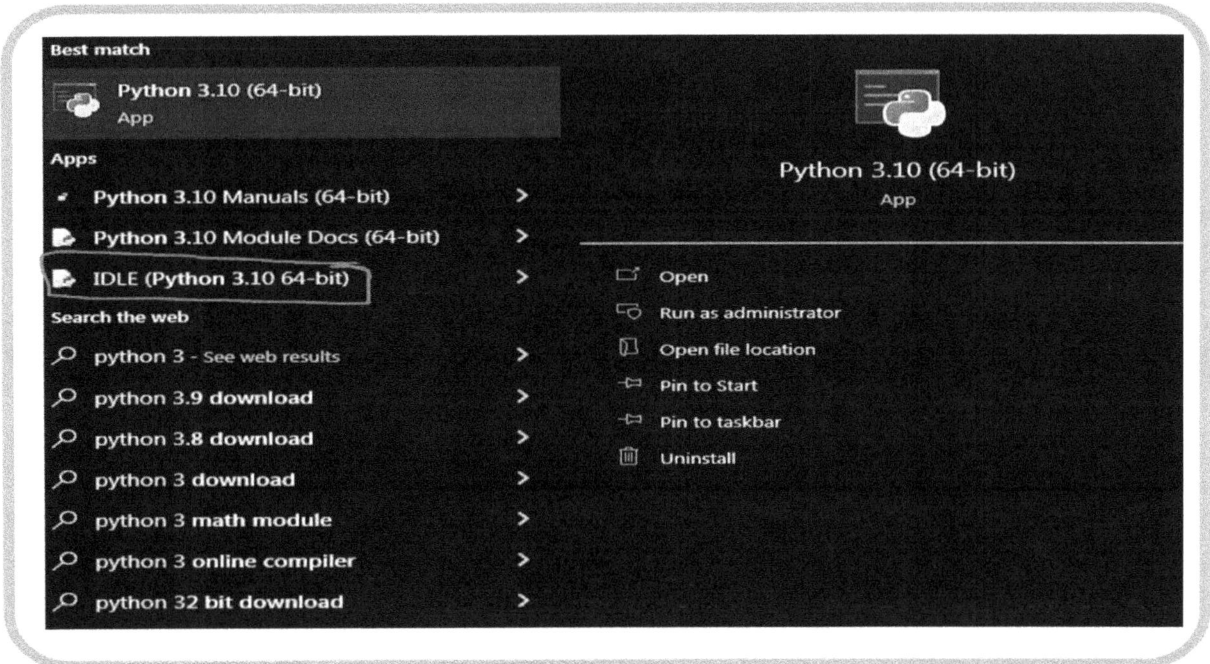

This starts the python shell.

```
IDLE Shell 3.10.2
File  Edit  Shell  Debug  Options  Window  Help
Python 3.10.2 (tags/v3.10.2:a58ebcc, Jan 17 2022, 14:12:15) [MSC v.1929 64 bit (
AMD64)] on win32
Type "help", "copyright", "credits" or "license()" for more information.
>>> |
```

Try to type the following commands

```
IDLE Shell 3.10.2
File  Edit  Shell  Debug  Options  Window  Help
Python 3.10.2 (tags/v3.10.2:a58ebcc, Jan 17 2022, 14:12:15) [MSC v.1929 64 bit (
AMD64)] on win32
Type "help", "copyright", "credits" or "license()" for more information.
>>> 10*20
200
>>> print("Welcome To Python Programming")
Welcome To Python Programming
>>> a=10
>>> b=20
>>> c=a+b
>>> print(c)
30
```

Inorder to do more elaborate programs,normally people store all the commands in a file.

To open a file to use in this way, goto File->New Window.

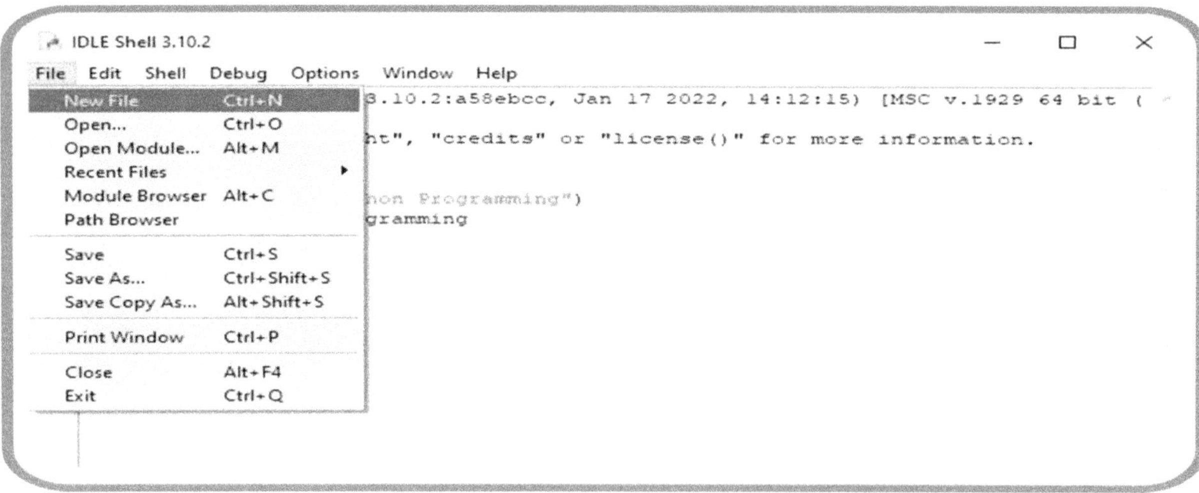

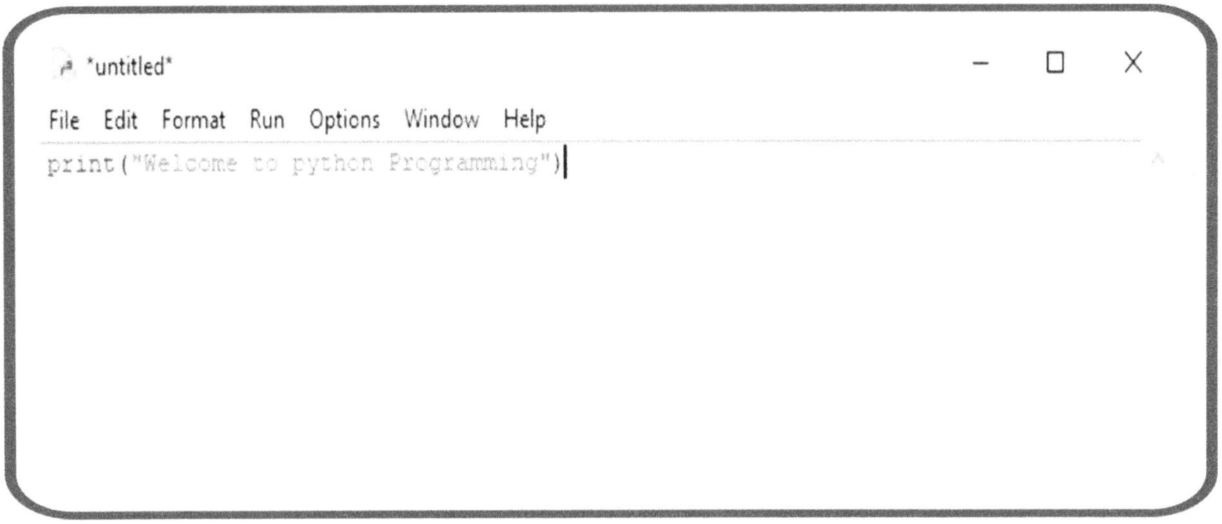
untitled
File Edit Format Run Options Window Help
print("Welcome to python Programming")

untitled
File Edit Format Run Options Window Help
New File Ctrl+N
Open... Ctrl+O
Open Module... Alt+M
Recent Files
Module Browser Alt+C
Path Browser
Save Ctrl+S
Save As... Ctrl+Shift+S
Save Copy As... Alt+Shift+S
Print Window Ctrl+P
Close Alt+F4
Exit Ctrl+Q
Programming")

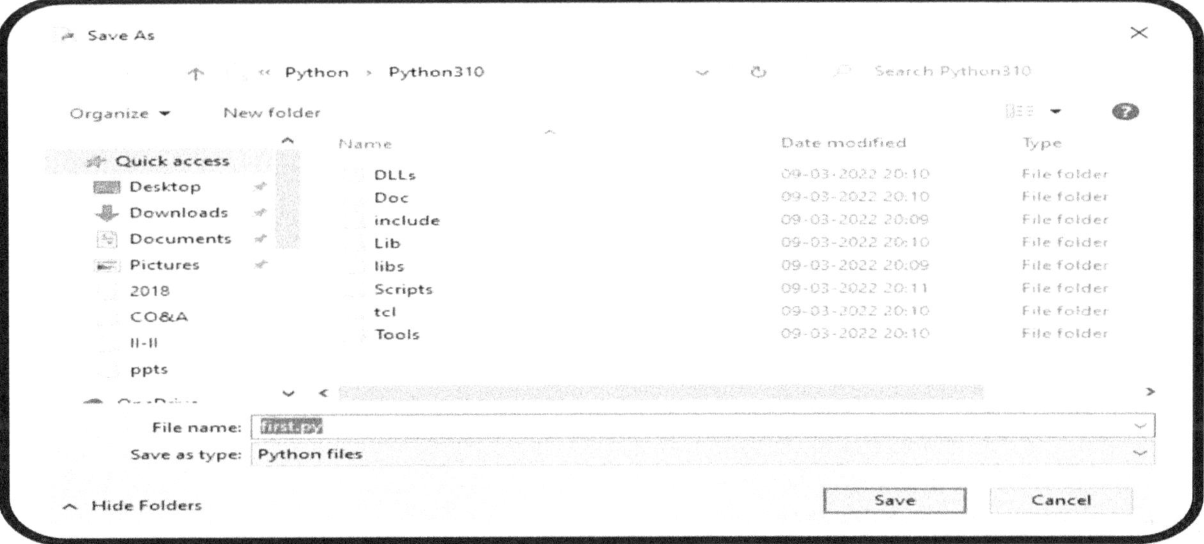
Save As
« Python › Python310
Search Python310
Organize
New folder
Quick access
Desktop
Downloads
Documents
Pictures
2018
CO&A
II-II
ppts
Name
Date modified
Type
DLLs 09-03-2022 20:10 File folder
Doc 09-03-2022 20:10 File folder
include 09-03-2022 20:09 File folder
Lib 09-03-2022 20:10 File folder
libs 09-03-2022 20:09 File folder
Scripts 09-03-2022 20:11 File folder
tcl 09-03-2022 20:10 File folder
Tools 09-03-2022 20:10 File folder
File name: first.py
Save as type: Python files
Hide Folders
Save
Cancel

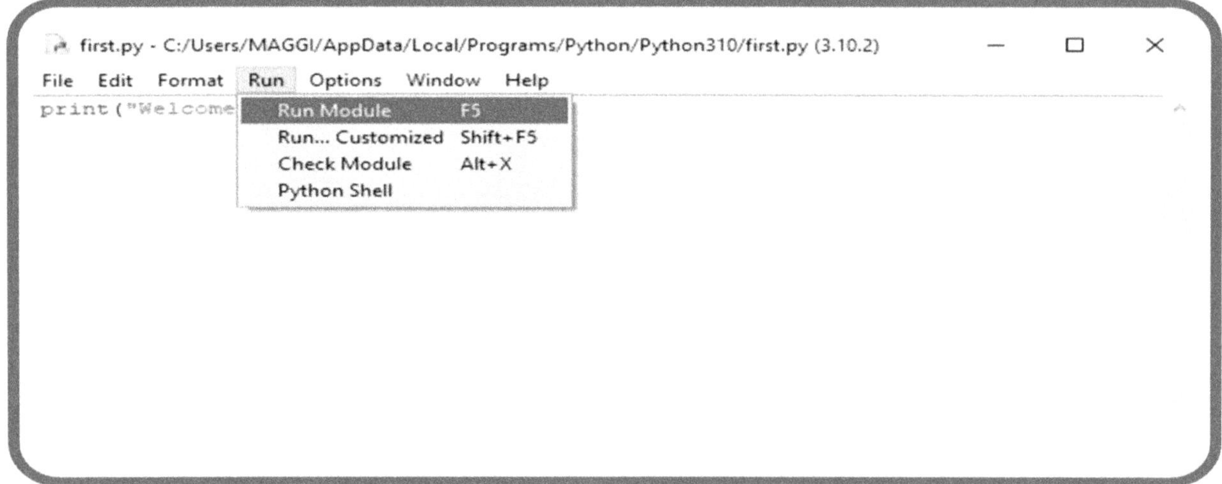

IDLE Shell 3.10.2

File Edit Shell Debug Options Window Help

```
Python 3.10.2 (tags/v3.10.2:a58ebcc, Jan 17 2022, 14:12:15) [MSC v.1929 64 bit (
AMD64)] on win32
Type "help", "copyright", "credits" or "license()" for more information.
>>>
=== RESTART: C:/Users/MAGGI/AppData/Local/Programs/Python/Python310/first.py ===
Welcome to python Programming
>>> |
```

4. Input and Output of Python:

- ✓ Python provides numerous built-in functions that are readily available to us at the Python prompt.
- ✓ Some of the functions like input() and print() are widely used for standard input and output operations respectively.

a) print() function:

It used to print the data into the standard output device (screen).

i)To display message into the screen

Syntax	**print('------------------------')**
Example	>>print('Welcome To Python')
Output	Welcome To Python

ii)To display values into the screen

Syntax	print(variable Name-1,Variable Nme-2,....)
Example	>>a=100 >>print(a)
Output	100

iii)To display message and value into the screen

Syntax	print('-----------------',variable Name)
Example	>>>a=50 >>> print('The value of a is', a)
Output	The value of a is 50

The actual syntax of the print() function is:

Syntax	print(objects, sep=' ', end='\n', file=sys.stdout, flush=False)
Example	>>>print(1, 2, 3, 4) >>>print(1, 2, 3, 4, sep='*') >>>print(1, 2, 3, 4, sep='#', end='&')
Output	1 2 3 4 1*2*3*4 1#2#3#4&

- ✓ Here, objects is the value(s) to be printed.
- ✓ The sep separator is used between the values. It defaults into a space character.
- ✓ After all values are printed, end is printed. It defaults into a new line.
- ✓ The file is the object where the values are printed and its default value is sys.stdout (screen). Here is an example to illustrate this.

Output formatting:

- ✓ Sometimes we would like to format our output to make it look attractive. This can be done by using the **str.format()** method. This method is visible to any string object.

Syntax	**str.format()**
Example	>>>x = 5; y = 10 >>>print('The value of x is {} and y is {}'.format(x,y))
Output	The value of x is 5 and y is 10

- ✓ Here, the curly braces {} are used as placeholders. We can specify the order in which they are printed by using numbers

Formatted output:

- ✓ Python's print statement, paired with the string format operator (%), supports string substitution, much like the printf()function in C

Example	**>>> print ("%s number %d " %("I am", 1))**
Output	I am number 1

Example	**>>>printf("%d is even number from %d to %d" % (4,1,10))**
Output	4 is even number from 1 to 10

b) input( ):

- ✓ Up until now, our programs were static. The value of variables was defined or hard coded into the source code.

- ✓ To allow flexibility, we might want to take the input from the user. In Python, we have the input() function to allow this.

- ✓ The easiest way to obtain user input from the command line is with the input() built-in function. It reads from standard input and assigns the string value to the variable

Syntax	**input(' --------------------- ')**
Example	>>>num = input('Enter a number: ')
Output	Enter a number: 10

- ✓ where dashed lines represents the string we wish to display on the screen. It is optional.
- ✓ Here, we can see that the entered value 10 is a string, not a number.
- ✓ To convert this into a number we can use int() or float() functions.

Note: The int() function converts the string num to an integer so that the mathematical operation can be performed.

>>>int('10') **10**	**>>> float('10')** **10.0**

Syntax	**int(input('----------------------------------'))**
Example	>>>num = int(input('Enter a number: '))
Output	Enter a number: 10

Example-1	**>>> print(input())**
Output	Hello Hello
Example-2	>>>x = input() >>>print("Your input is: ", x)

Output	Hello Your input is: Hello
Example-3	>>>val1 = input("Enter a value: ") >>>val2 = input("Enter another value: ") >>>print("val1 =", val1) >>>print("val2 =", val2)
Output	Enter a value: 10 Enter another value: 3.4 val1 = 10 val2 = 3.4

5. Comment Line in Python:

- ✓ A comment begins with a hash character(#) which is not a part of the string literal and continues until the end of the line.
- ✓ All characters after the # character up to the end of the line are part of the comment and the Python interpreter ignores them.
- ✓ Note that Python has no multi- lines or block comments facility.

Example	>>> x=1 #Value 1 is assigned to x

6. Joining two lines:

- ✓ In Python, a backslash (\) is a continuation character, and if it is placed at the end of a line, it is considered that the line is continued, ignoring subsequent newlines.
- ✓ When you want to write a long code in a single line you can break the line in two or more physical lines using backslash character(\)

Example	**>>>n = 1 + 2 ** **+ 3**

	>>>print(n)
Output	6

7. Multiple Statements on a Single Line:

- ✓ Normally each statement is written on separate physical line in editor.You can write two separate statements into a single line using a semicolon (;) character between two line.

Example	**a=10** **b=20** **c=a*b** **print (c)**
Example	**a=10; b=20; c=1*b; print (c)**

8. Indentation in Python:

- ✓ Indentation refers to the spaces at the beginning of a code line.
- ✓ Python uses whitespace (spaces and tabs) to define program blocks
- ✓ Whereas other languages like C, C++ use braces ({}) to indicate blocks of codes for class, functions or flow control.
- ✓ The number of whitespaces (spaces and tabs) in the indentation is not fixed, but all statements within the block must be the indented same amount.
- ✓ The indentation in Python is very important. Python uses indentation to indicate a block of code.

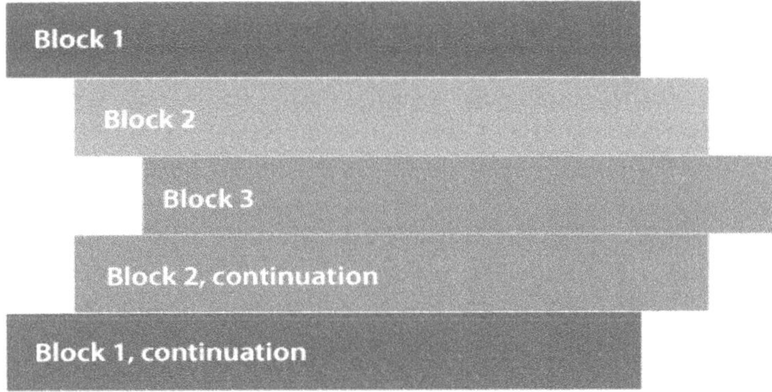

Without indentation	if 5 > 2: print("Five is greater than two!")
With indentation	if 5 > 2: print("Five is greater than two!")

Example-1(Without indentation) will give you an error if you skip the indentation.

9. Python Keywords:

- ✓ Python has a set of keywords that are reserved words that cannot be used as variable names, function names, or any other identifiers.
- ✓ In Python 3.6, there are 33 reserved keywords:

Keywords

False	elif	lambda
None	else	nonlocal
True	except	not
and	finally	or
as	for	pass
assert	from	raise
break	global	return
class	if	try
continue	import	while
def	in	with
del	is	yield

10. Variables in Python:

- ✓ A variable is a memory location where a programmer can store a value.
- ✓ Python has no command for declaring a variable.
- ✓ A variable is created the moment you first assign a value to it.
- ✓ Variables do not need to be declared with any particular type, and can even change type after they have been set.

>>>x = 8 # x is of type int >>>x = "CSE" # x is now of type string >>>print(x)	>>>x = 8 # x is of type int >>>y = "Ram" # y is of type string >>>print(x) >>>print(y)

10.1 Rules for construction of Variable Name:

- ✓ Variable name must begin with a letter (a - z, A - B) or underscore (_).
- ✓ Other characters can be letters, numbers or underscore.
- ✓ Variable names are case sensitive.
- ✓ Variable names can be any (reasonable) length.
- ✓ There are some reserved words which you cannot use as a variable name because Python uses them for other things.

10.2 Assigning Value to Variable:

(i) Assignment of Single Value:

Here the equal sign (=) is used to assign right side value to a variable.

Syntax	**<variable> = <expr>**
Example	>>> a=10

(ii) Assignment of Multiple Values:

We can also assign a single value to more than one variables simultaneously.

Syntax	**var1=var2=var3...varn = <expr>**
Example	**>>> a=b=c=d=10** **>>>print(a); print(b);print(c); print(d);**

(iii)Assigning different values:

Here, the variables assign many values at the same time.

Syntax	**<var>, <var>, ..., <var> = <expr>, <expr>, ...,<expr>**
Example	>>>x, y, z = 10, 1.2, “EEE"

11. Operators:

Def: Operators are special symbols in Python that carry out arithmetic or logical computation.

✓ The value that the operator operates on is called the operand.

✓ Operators are used to perform operations on variables and values. Python divides the operators in the following groups:

- ❖ Arithmetic operators
- ❖ Assignment operators
- ❖ Comparison operators
- ❖ Logical operators
- ❖ Identity operators
- ❖ Membership operators
- ❖ Bitwise operators

i)Arithmetic operators:

✓ Arithmetic operators are used to perform arithmetic operations between two operands.

✓ It uses the numeric values to perform common mathematical operations

Operator	**Name**	**Example**
+	Addition	x + y
-	Subtraction	x – y
*	Multiplication	x * y
/	Division	x / y
%	Modulus	x % y
**	Exponentiation	x ** y
//	Floor division	x // y

Program	Output
# Exampleof ArithmeticOperators	x + y = 19
x = 15	x - y = 11
y = 4	x * y = 60
print('x + y =',x+y)	x / y = 3.75
print('x - y =',x-y)	x // y = 3
print('x * y =',x*y)	x ** y = 50625
print('x / y =',x/y)	
print('x // y =',x//y)	
print('x ** y =',x**y)	

ii)Assignment operators:

- ✓ Assignment operators are used to assign values to variables.
- ✓ Simple assignment operator that assigns the value on the right to the variable a on the left.
- ✓ There are various compound operators in Python like += ,-=,*= that performs the operation and later assigns the value to variable.

Operator	Name	Equivalent to
=	x = 5	x = 5
+=	x += 5	x = x + 5
-=	x -= 5	x = x – 5
*=	x *= 5	x = x * 5
/=	x /= 5	x = x / 5
%=	x %= 5	x = x % 5
//=	x //= 5	x = x // 5
**=	x **= 5	x = x ** 5
&=	x &= 5	x = x & 5

|=	x |= 5	x = x | 5
^=	x ^= 5	x = x ^ 5
>>=	x >>= 5	x = x >> 5
<<=	x <<= 5	x = x << 5

Program	Output
# Examples of Assignment Operators	10
a = 10	20
b = a	10
print(b)	100
b += a	102400
print(b)	
b -= a	
print(b)	
b *= a	
print(b)	
b <<= a	
print(b)	

iii)Comparison operators:

- ✓ Comparison operators are used to compare two values.
- ✓ It either returns True or False according to the condition.

Operator	Name	Example
==	Equal	x == y
!=	Not equal	x != y

>	Greater than	x > y
<	Less than	x < y
>=	Greater than or equal to	x >= y
<=	Less than or equal to	x <= y

Program	Output
# Example of Comparison Operators	
a = 10	False
b = 20	True
print(a > b)	False
print(a < b)	True
print(a == b)	False
print(a != b)	True
print(a >= b)	
print(a <= b)	

iv)Logical operators:

- ✓ Logical operators are used to combine conditional statements.
- ✓ Theses operators are used primarily in the expression evaluation to make a decision

Operator	Name	Example
and	Returns True if both statements are true	x < 5 and x < 10
Or	Returns True if one of the statements is true	x < 5 or x < 4
Not	Reverse the result, returns False if the result is true	not(x < 5 and x < 10)

Program	Output

# Example of Logical Operator 	
x = True
y = False
print(x and y)
print(x or y)
print(not x)
	False
	True
	False

v) Identity operators:

- ✓ Identity operators are used to compare the objects, not if they are equal, but if they are actually the same object, with the same memory location.
- ✓ "is" and "is not" are the identity operators in Python. They are used to check if two values (or variables) are located on the same part of the memory.
- ✓ Two variables that are equal does not imply that they are identical.

Operator	Name	Example
is	Returns True if both variables are the same object	x is y
is not	Returns True if both variables are not the same object	x is not y

Program	Output

# Example of Identity Operator 	
a = 10
b = 20
c = a
print(a is not b)
	True
	True

print(a is c)	

vi) Membership operators:

- ✓ Python membership operators are used to check the membership of value inside a Python data structure. If the value is present in the data structure, then the resulting value is true otherwise it returns false.
- ✓ "in" and "not in" are the membership operators in Python. They are used to test whether a value or variable is found in a sequence (string, list, tuple, set and dictionary).

Operator	**Name**	**Example**
in	Returns True if a sequence with the specified value is present in the object	x in y
not in	Returns True if a sequence with the specified value is not present in the object	x not in y

Program	**Output**
# Example of membership Operator **x = 14** **y = 50** **list = [10, 20, 30, 40, 50]** **if (x not in list):** **print("x is NOT present in given list")** **else:**	**x is NOT present in given list** **y is present in given list**

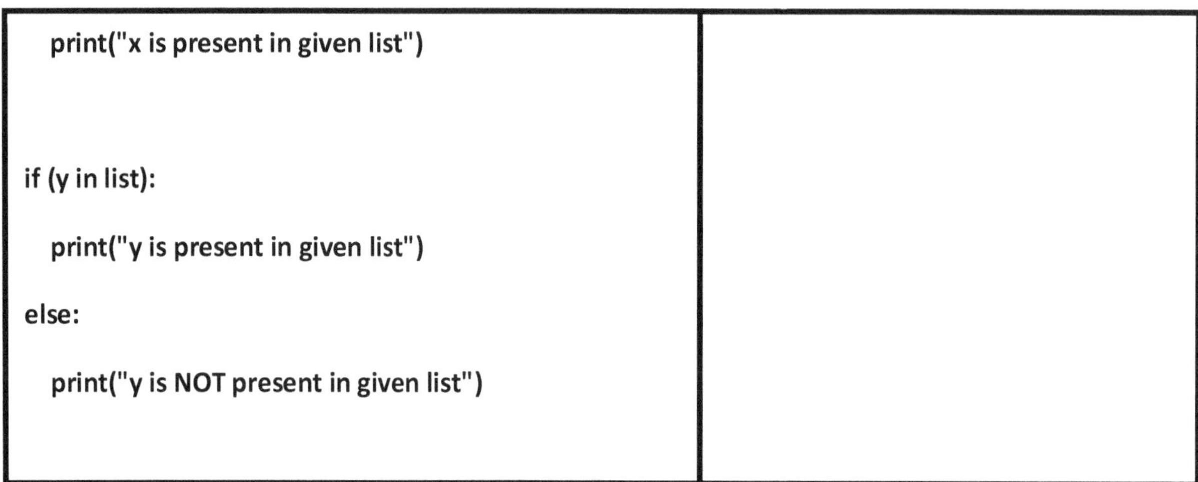

```
    print("x is present in given list")


if (y in list):
    print("y is present in given list")
else:
    print("y is NOT present in given list")
```

vii) Bitwise operators:

Bitwise operators are used to compare (binary) numbers. The bitwise operators perform bit by bit operation on the values of the two operands.

Operator	Name	Example
&	Bitwise AND	x & y = 0 (0000 0000)
|	Bitwise OR	x | y = 14 (0000 1110)
~	Bitwise NOT	~x = -11 (1111 0101)
^	Bitwise XOR	x ^ y = 14 (0000 1110)
>>	Bitwise right shift	x >> 2 = 2 (0000 0010)
<<	Bitwise left shift	x << 2 = 40 (0010 1000)

Program	Output
# Examples of Bitwise operators	0
a = 10	14
b = 4	-11
print(a & b)	14
print(a | b)	2

print(~a) print(a ^ b) print(a >> 2) print(a << 2)	40

12. Expressions:

- ✓ An expression is a combination of operators and operands that is interpreted to produce some other value.
- ✓ In any programming language, an expression is evaluated as per the precedence of its operators.
- ✓ So that if there is more than one operator in an expression, their precedence decides which operation will be performed first.
- ✓ Example: x = 5, y = 3, z = x + y
- ✓ In the above example x, y and z are variables, 5 and 3 are values, = and + are operators.

13. Decision Making Statements /Conditional Statements:

- ✓ Decision making is the most important aspect of almost all the programming languages.
- ✓ Decision making is required when we want to execute a code only if a certain condition is satisfied.
- ✓ As the name implies, decision making allows us to run a particular block of code for a particular decision.
- ✓ Here, the decisions are made on the validity of the particular conditions.
- ✓ Python supports different decision making statements,They are:

(i) if Statement:

Syntax	Flow Chart
if Condition: statement(s)	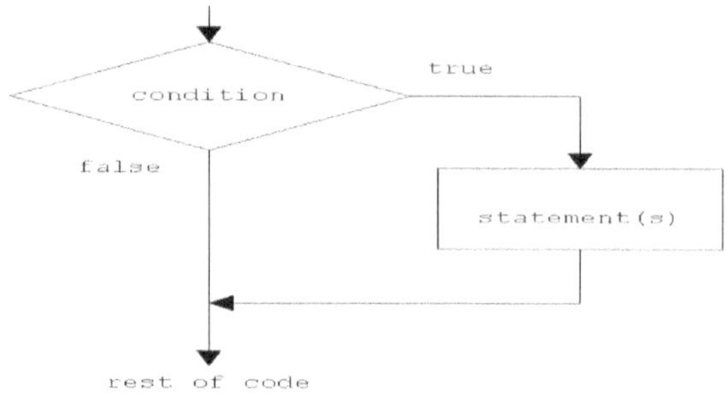 condition true false statement(s) rest of code

- ✓ Here,if statement is used to test a particular condition and if the condition is true, it executes a block of code known as if-block.
- ✓ If the condition is False, the statement(s) is not executed.
- ✓ In Python, the body of the if statement is indicated by the indentation. The body starts with an indentation and the first unindented line marks the end.

Program	Output

# Example of simple if statement 	
num = int(input("enter the number: "))
if num%2 == 0:
   print("Number is even")
	enter the number: 8
	Number is even

(ii) if - else Statement:

Syntax	Flow Chart

If Condition:
  #Body of if
else:
  #Body of else
	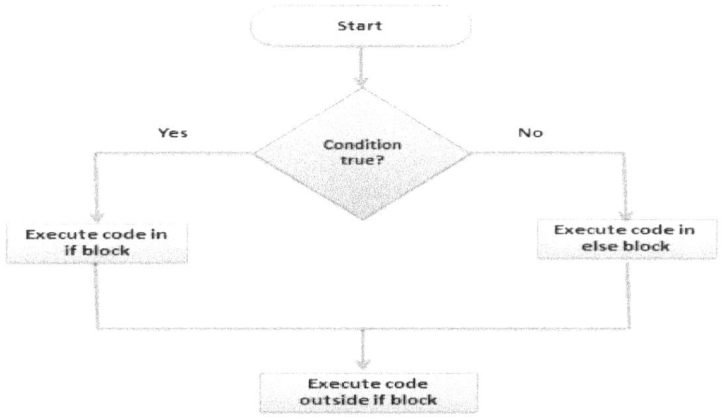 Start
	Condition true?
	Yes
	No
	Execute code in if block
	Execute code in else block
	Execute code outside if block

- ✓ The if-else statement provides an else block combined with the if statement which is executed in the false case of the condition.
- ✓ If the condition is true, then the if-block is executed. Otherwise, the else-block is executed.

Program	Output

# Example of if else statement 	
num = int(input("enter the number:"))
if num%2 == 0:
  print("Number is even")
else:
  print("Number is odd")
	enter the number: 51
	Number is odd

(iii) elif statement:

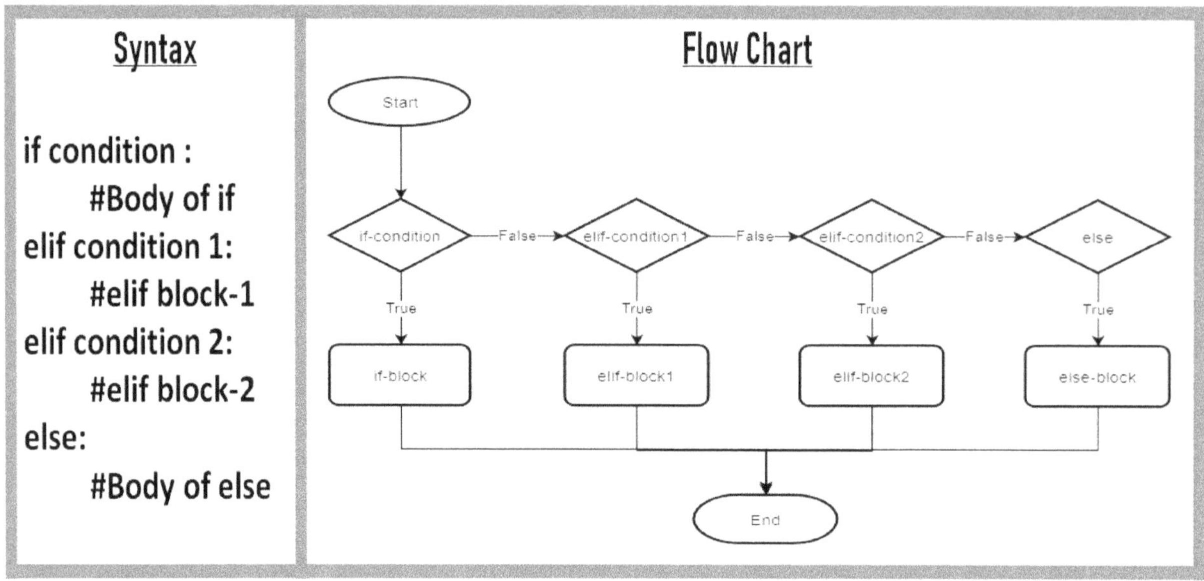

✓ In this case, the If condition is evaluated first. If it is false, the elif statement will be executed; if it also comes false, the Else statement will be executed.

Program	Output

# Example of elif statement 	
age =int(input('Enter your age:'))
if age < 5:
ticket_price = 5
elif age < 16:
ticket_price = 10
else:
ticket_price = 18
print("You'll pay ${ticket_price} for the ticket")
	Enter your age:15
	You'll pay $10 for the ticket

(iv) Nested if statement:

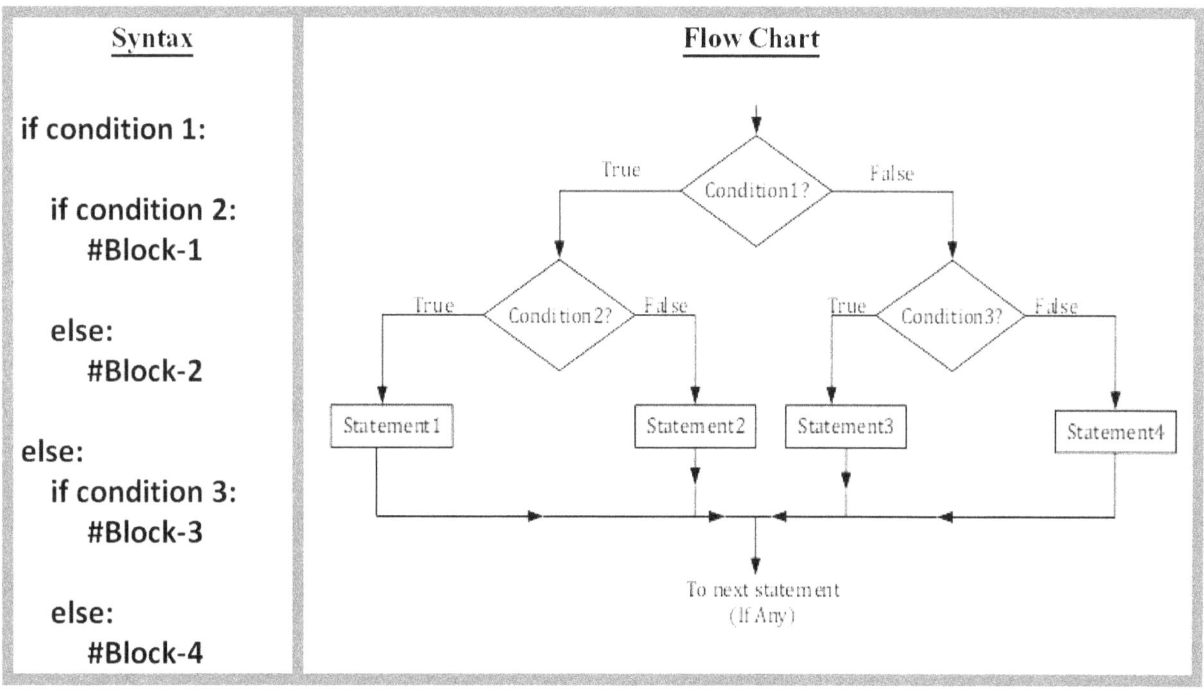

Program	Output
# Example of nested if statement	Enter A: 13
a=int(input("Enter A: "))	Enter B: 22
b=int(input("Enter B: "))	Enter C: 8
c=int(input("Enter C: "))	Greater = 22

```
# Example of  nested if statement
a=int(input("Enter A: "))
b=int(input("Enter B: "))
c=int(input("Enter C: "))
if a>b:
    if a>c:
        g=a
    else:
        g=c
else:
    if b>c:
        g=b
    else:
        g=c
```

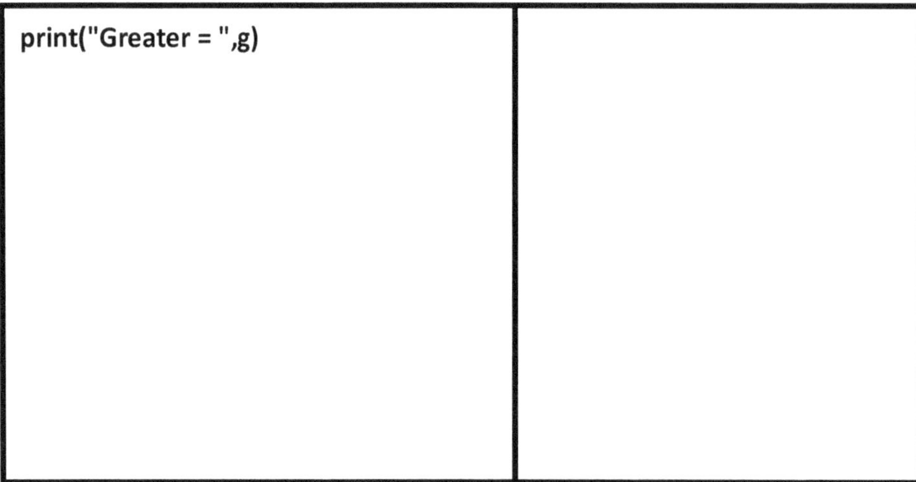

print("Greater = ",g)	

14. Loops:

(i) for loop:

- ✓ The for loop in Python is used to iterate over a sequence (list, tuple, string) or other iterable objects. Iterating over a sequence is called traversal.

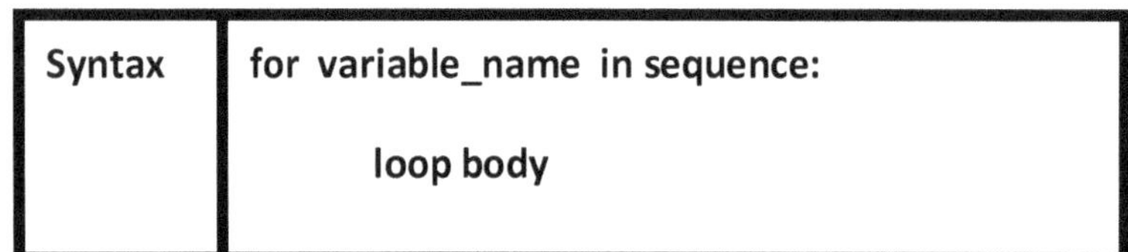

Syntax	for variable_name in sequence: loop body

- ✓ Here, the variable takes the value of the item inside the sequence on each iteration.
- ✓ Loop continues until we reach the last item in the sequence. The body of for loop is separated from the rest of the code using indentation.

Operation of for Loop

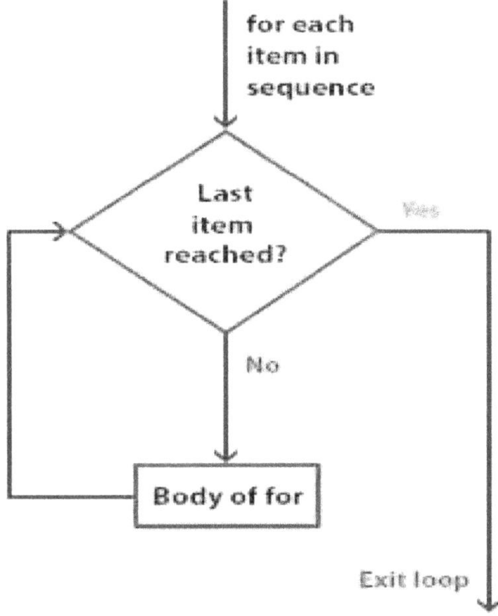

Program	Output

# Program to find the sum of all numbers stored in a list 	
num = [6, 5, 3, 8, 4, 2, 5, 4, 11]
sum = 0
for i in num:
    sum = sum + i
print("The sum is", sum)
	The sum is 48

range() function:

- ✓ We can generate a sequence of numbers using range() function.

Ex:range(10) will generate numbers from 0 to 9 (10 numbers).

- ✓ We can also define the start, stop and step size as range(start, stop, stepsize). Step size defaults to 1 if not provided.
- ✓ This function does not store all the values in memory; it would be inefficient. So it remembers the start, stop, step size and generates the next number on the go.

Syntax	for variable_name in range(start, stop, stepsize): loop body	Output 2 3 4 5
Example	for x in range(2, 6): print(x)	

Program Iterating string using for loop str = "Python" for i in str: print(i)	Output P y t h o n

Program to print numbers in sequence for i in range(10): print(i,end = ' ')	Output 0 1 2 3 4 5 6 7 8 9

Program to print table of given number n = int(input("Enter the number ")) for i in range(1,11): c = n*i print(n,"*",i,"=",c)	Output Enter the number 10 10 * 1 = 10 10 * 2 = 20 10 * 3 = 30 10 * 4 = 40 10 * 5 = 50 10 * 6 = 60 10 * 7 = 70 10 * 8 = 80

	10 * 9 = 90 10 * 10 = 100

Nested for loop in python:

- ✓ Python allows us to nest any number of for loops inside a for loop. The inner loop is executed n number of times for every iteration of the outer loop.
- ✓ The syntax is:

Syntax	<pre>**for** var1 **in** sequence: #outer loop
	   for var2 **in** sequence: #inner loop
	      #block of statements
	#Other statements</pre>
		Output
		
		1
		
		22
		
		333
		
		4444
		
		55555

Example	n = int(input("Enter the rows"))
	for i **in** range(0,n+1):
	   for j **in** range(i):
	      print(i,end = '')
	   print()	

(ii) while loop:

- ✓ Python while loop allows a part of the code to be executed until the given condition returns false. It is also known as a pre-tested loop.

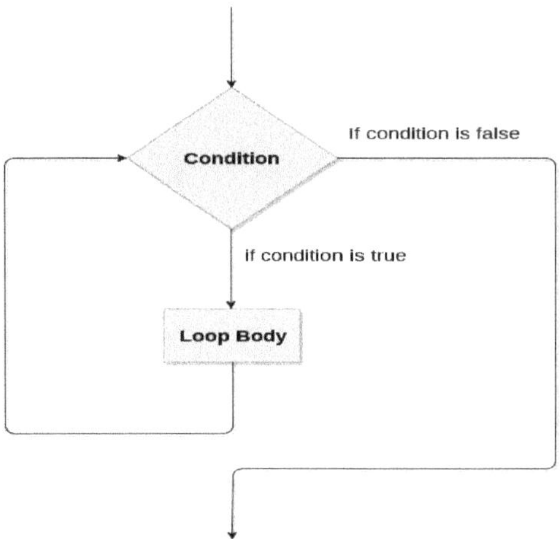

Syntax	while expression: statements	Output 1 2 3 4 5
Example	i = 1 while i < 6: print(i) i = i+1	

15. Loop Control Statements:

- ✓ We can change the normal sequence of loop's execution using the loop control statement.
- ✓ When the loop's execution is completed, all automatic objects defined in that scope are demolished.
- ✓ Python offers the following control statement to use within the loop.

(i) **Continue Statement :** When the continue statement is encountered, the control transfer to the beginning of the loop.

Syntax	Example	Output
....	i = 0	1
continue	while i < 6:	2
....	i += 1	4
	if i == 3:	5

	continue print(i)	6

(ii) **break Statement:**When the break statement is encountered, it brings control out of the loop.

Syntax	Example	Output

………………
break
………………
………………
	i = 1
	while i < 6:
	print(i)
	if (i == 3):
	break
	i =i+1
		1
		2
		3

(iii) Pass Statement: The pass statement is used to declare the empty loop. It is also used to define empty class, function, and control statement. Let's understand the following example.

Syntax	Example	Output
……………… **pass** ……………… ………………	for x in [0, 1, 2]: pass	

2. Data Types

1. Data Types:

- ✓ In programming, data type is an important concept.
- ✓ Variables can store data of different types, and different types can do different things.
- ✓ Python is a dynamically typed language; hence we do not need to define the type of the variable while declaring it. The interpreter implicitly binds the value with its type.
- ✓ Every value in Python has a datatype. Since everything is an object in Python programming, data types are actually classes and variables are instance (object) of these classes.
- ✓ Python has the following data types built-in by default, in these categories:

i.	Text Type	:str
ii.	Numeric Types	:int, float, complex
iii.	Sequence Types	:list, tuple, range
iv.	Mapping Type	:dict
v.	Set Types	:set, frozenset
vi.	Boolean Type	:bool
vii.	Binary Types	:bytes, bytearray, memoryview

1.1 Immutable Definition:

- ✓ Immutable is the when no change is possible over time. In Python, if the value of an object cannot be changed over time, then it is known as immutable. Once created, the value of these objects is permanent.
- ✓ Objects of built-in type that are immutable are:
    - Numbers (Integer, Rational, Float, Decimal, Complex & Booleans)
    - Strings
    - Tuples
    - Frozen Sets
    - User-Defined Classes (It purely depends upon the user to define the characteristics)

1.2 Mutable Definition:

- ✓ Mutable is when something is changeable or has the ability to change. In Python, 'mutable' is the ability of objects to change their values. These are often the objects that store a collection of data.
- ✓ List of Mutable objects are:
    - Lists
    - Sets
    - Dictionaries
    - User-Defined Classes (It purely depends upon the user to define the characteristics)

1.3 Objects in Python

- ✓ In Python, everything is treated as an object. Every object has these three attributes:
- ✓ ***Identity:*** This refers to the address that the object refers to in the computer's memory.
- ✓ ***Type***: This refers to the kind of object that is created. For example- integer, list, string etc.
- ✓ ***Value***: This refers to the value stored by the object. For example – List=[1,2,3] would hold the numbers 1,2 and 3.

1.4 Getting the Data Type:

- ✓ Python also enables us to check the data-type of the variables through which we can know which data-type value the variable is holding in the program.
- ✓ You can get the data type of any object by using the **type()** function.
- ✓ Consider the following example to define the values of different data types and checking its type.

Example	Output
a=10 b="Hi Python" c = 10.5 print(type(a)) print(type(b)) print(type(c))	<class 'int'> <class 'str'> <class 'float'>

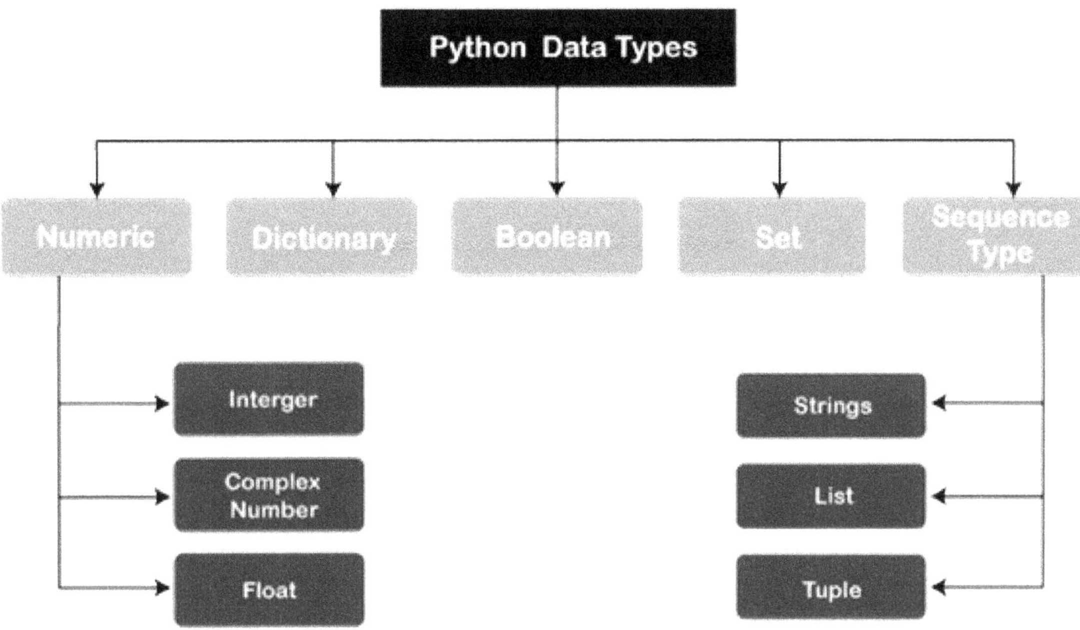

2. Numeric Data-Type:

- ✓ Python supports the following three types of numeric data-type:
    - ***Int (Integer)***
    - ***Float***
    - ***Complex Number***
- ✓ It is to be noted that Python does not support any special numeric data-type such as long int or double etc.

2.1 Integer data-type:

- ✓ Variables with int data-type inside Python hold integer number objects. These integer number objects can be 10, 200, -30, -700 etc.
- ✓ In Python, there is no restriction for the length of an integer number.
- ✓ A variable with an integer data-type can hold a maximum value integer number. The value of integer number belongs to int.

Example	Output
i = 27 print("The type of i",type(i))	The type of i <class 'int‘>

- ✓ We can say that the sign of numbers (negative or positive) or length of numbers, the data-type of the variable will be int only.

2.2 Float data-type:

- ✓ In Python, the variables having float data-type represent that they are holding floating-point numbers objects such as 1.9, 2.34, 3.14 etc.
- ✓ The decimal limit of float data-type is up to 15 decimal points in Python.
- ✓ It means float data-type variables have accurate and precise object values up to 15 decimal points. Variables with both positive and negative numbers can have float data-type in Python.

Example	Output
j = -2.34 print("The type of j",type(j))	The type of j <class 'float'>

2.3 Complex number data-type:

- ✓ A complex number has two parts, i.e., real and imaginary, and has the structure same as a+ib.
- ✓ Here, 'a' represents the real part of the complex number, and 'ib' represents the real part of the complex number.
- ✓ The variables which hold complex numbers have complex data-type in Python.
- ✓ Example: 2+3i, 2.3+1.2i, 0.23i etc.

Example	Output
c = 2.3+0.23i print(c) print(type(c))	2.3+0.23i <class 'complex'>

Note: A variable which is storing number having only real part is also considered as complex data-type. Let's clear this through an example

Example	Output
a = 5 print(a, "is of type", type(a)) a = 2.0 print(a, "is of type", type(a)) a = 1+2j print(a, "is complex number?", isinstance(1+2j,complex))	5 is of type <class 'int'> 2.0 is of type <class 'float'> (1+2j) is complex number? True

2.4 Complex numbers built in attributes

Attribute	Description
num.real	Real component of complex number num
num.imag	Imaginary component of complex number num
num.conjugate()	Returns complex conjugate of num

```
>>> acomplex=8.3+1.4j
>>> acomplex
(8.3+1.4j)
>>> acomplex.real
8.3
>>> acomplex.imag
1.4
>>> acomplex.conjugate()
(8.3-1.4j)
>>>
```

2.5 Mixed-Mode Operations

- ✓ If both numbers are the same type, no conversion is necessary. Therules of coercion follow from these two examples: integers movetowardfloat,andallmovetowardcomplex.
- ✓ Ifeitherargumentisacomplexnumber,theotherisconvertedto complex;
- ✓ Otherwise,ifeitherargumentisafloatingpointnumber,theother isconvertedtofloatingpoint;
- ✓ Otherwise,ifeitherargumentisalong,theotherisconvertedto long;
- ✓ Otherwise, both must be plainintegers and no conversion is necessary.
- ✓ The following is an example showing you Python's automatic coercion.
- ✓ In order to add the numbers (one integer, one float), both need to be converted to the same type.
- ✓ Since float is the superset, the integer is coerced to a float before the operation happens, leaving the result as a float:

>>> 1 + 4.5

5.5

2.6 Conversion Factory Functions:

- ✓ The int(), long(), float(), and complex() functions are used to convert from any numeric type to another.

Example

>>> int(4.25555)

4

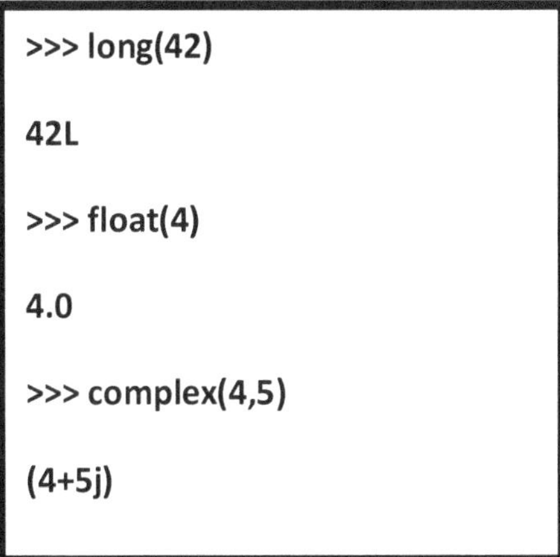

```
>>> long(42)
42L
>>> float(4)
4.0
>>> complex(4,5)
(4+5j)
```

2.7 Numbers and built-in functions:

(i)abs(): Thisfunction is used to return the absolute value of a number

Example	Output
a = -20 print('Absolute value of -20 is:', abs(a))	Absolute value of -20 is: 20
f = -20.83 print('Absolute value of -20.83 is:', abs(f))	Absolute value of -20.83 is: 20.83

(ii)bin() : This function is used to return the binary representation of a specified integer. A result always starts with the prefix 0b.

Example	Output
x = 10 y = bin(x) print (y)	0b1010

(iii)bool(): It converts a value to boolean(True or False) using the standard truth testing procedure.

Example x = bool(1) print(x)	Example y=bool(0) print(y)
Output True	Output False

(v)exec(): This function is used for the dynamic execution of Python program which can either be a string or object code and it accepts large blocks of code, unlike the eval() function which only accepts a single expression.

prog = 'print("The sum of 5 and 10 is", (5+10)) exec(prog)
15

(vi)sum(): This function is used to get the sum of numbers of an iterable, i.e., list.

Example List=[1,2,3] list2=[2,3,4] s = sum(list) R=sum(list2) Print(r) print(s)	Output -7 9

(vii)any() : This function returns true if any item in an iterable is true. Otherwise, it returns False.

Example mylist = [ ] x = any(mylist)	Output false

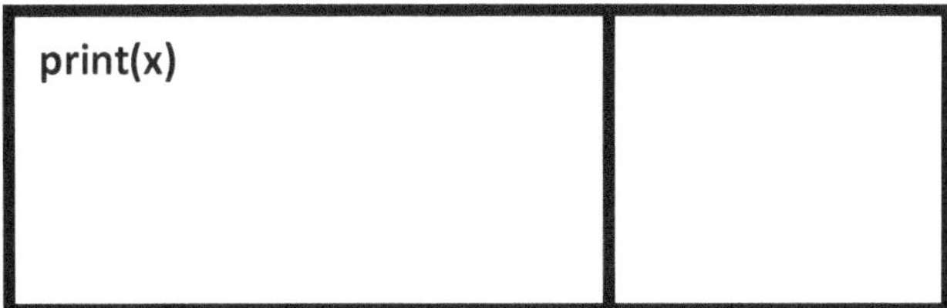

(viii)ascii(): This function returns a string containing a printable representation of an object and escapes the non-ASCII characters in the string using \x, \u or \U escapes.

normalText = 'Python is interesting' print(ascii(normalText))
Python is interesting

3. Sequence Data-type:

- ✓ In Python, the sequence data-type is an ordered or paired collection of similar or different data values. The sequence data-type allows us to store multiple object values in an efficient and organized manner.
- ✓ Variables with sequence data-type in Python are used to store values with characters, alphabets, words, lists etc.
- ✓ Like numeric data-type, sequence data-type also has three further data-types.
- ✓ Following are the three types of sequence data-type present in Python:
    - ***String***
    - ***List***
    - ***Tuple***
- ✓ Let's discuss each of these three data-types in detail.

3.1 String:

- ✓ A string in Python can be defined as a sequence of characters (including white spaces) represented inside the quotation marks. A variable storing a string object value is considered a string data-type. In Python, we can define string object value using single, double or triple quotation marks.

- ✓ We can also define a multiline string using triple quotes at the beginning of the string and end our string in the next line by closing it with triple quotation marks.

Let's understand this string data-type through an example.

Example	Output
mkr = "A string object " print(mkr) str = '''This is a multiline string''' print(str)	A string object This is a multiline string

- ✓ In the above code, we have defined a string mkr inside the double quotation mark. Then we defined multiline string str using five quotation marks and closed the string in the next line.

3.1.1 How to Update Strings:

- ✓ You can "update" an existing string by (re)assigning a variable to another string.
- ✓ The new value can be related to its previous value or to a completely different string altogether.

s = "helo"   want to change to"help!"

s[3] = "p" — error!

```
>>> aString = aString[:6] + 'Python!'      #use slices and concatenation
>>> aString
```

Output

'Hello Python!'

3.1.2 How to Remove Characters in a String:

Strings are immutable, so you cannot remove individual characters

from an existing string.

Ex: To remove one letter from "Hello World!"...the (lowercase) letter "l,"

Example	Output

>>> aString = 'Hello World!'
>>> aString = aString[:3] + aString[4:]
>>> aString
	'Helo World!'

3.1.3 Deleting a string:

✓ To clear or remove a string, you assign an empty string or use the del

statement, respectively

Example

>>> aString = 'h '
>>> aString 'h '
>>> del aString

3.1.4 String Handling in Python:

S.No.	Syntax	Description	Example	Output
1	lower()	we will convert all the characters as lower case in the string	>>> a='Book' >>> a.lower()	book
2	upper ()	we will convert all the characters as upper case in the string	>>> a='book' >>> a.upper()	BOOK
3	len()	The len() function returns the length of a string	>>> a='book' >>> len(a)	4
4	str()	This function converts any data type into a string	>>> str(2+3j)	'(2+3j)'
5	strip()	It removes whitespaces	>>> a=' Book '	Book

		from the beginning and end of the string	>>> a.strip()	
6	isdigit()	Returns True if all characters in a string are digits	>>> a='777' >> a.isdigit()	TRUE
			>>> a='77a' >>> a.isdigit()	FALSE
7	isalpha()	Returns True if all characters in a string are characters from an alphabet	>>> a='abc' >>> a.isalpha()	TRUE
8	isspace()	Returns True if all characters in a string are spaces.	>>> a=' ' >>> a.isspace()	TRUE
9	find()	It takes an argument and searches for it in the string on which it is applied. It then returns the index of the substring.	>>> 'homeowner'.find('meow')	2
10	replace()	It takes two arguments. The first is the substring to be replaced. The second is the substring to replace with.	>>> 'banana'.replace('na','ha')	Bahaha
11	split()	It takes one argument. The string is then split around every occurrence of the argument in the string.	>>> 'No. Okay. Why?'.split('.')	['No', ' Okay', ' Why?']

12	join()	It takes a list as an argument and joins the elements in the list using the string it is applied on	**>>> "*".join(['red','green','blue'])**	red*green*blue
13	isalnum( )	Returns True if the string contains only letters and digit. It returns False. If the string contains any special character like _, @, #, ", etc.	**>>>str1='Save Earth'**	FALSE
			>>>strl.isalnum()	(The function returns False as space)
14	swapcase( )	It will change case of every character to its opposite case vice-versa.	**>>> strl="tAmiL NaDu"**	TaMIl nAdU
			>>> print(strl.swapcase())	
15	capitalize( )	Used to capitalize the first character of the string	**>>> city="hyderbad"**	Hyderbad
			>>> print(city.capitalize())	
16	find(sub k start[, end]])	The function is used to search the first occurrence of the sub string in the given string. It returns the index at which the substring starts. It returns -1 if the substring does not	**>>>strl.'mammals'**	0
			>>>strl.fmd(`ma)	

- ✓ Python also provides us many operators for performing various operations on the string.
- ✓ In a string handling case, the '+' character (string addition operator) is used to concatenate(add) two string values. As in this operation, "Hi" + "Python Developers" will return "Hi Python Developers" as a single string to us.
- ✓ The '*' character (string multiple operators) is also known as the repetition operator for strings. As in this operator, "Hello"*2 will return 'HelloHello' in the output.

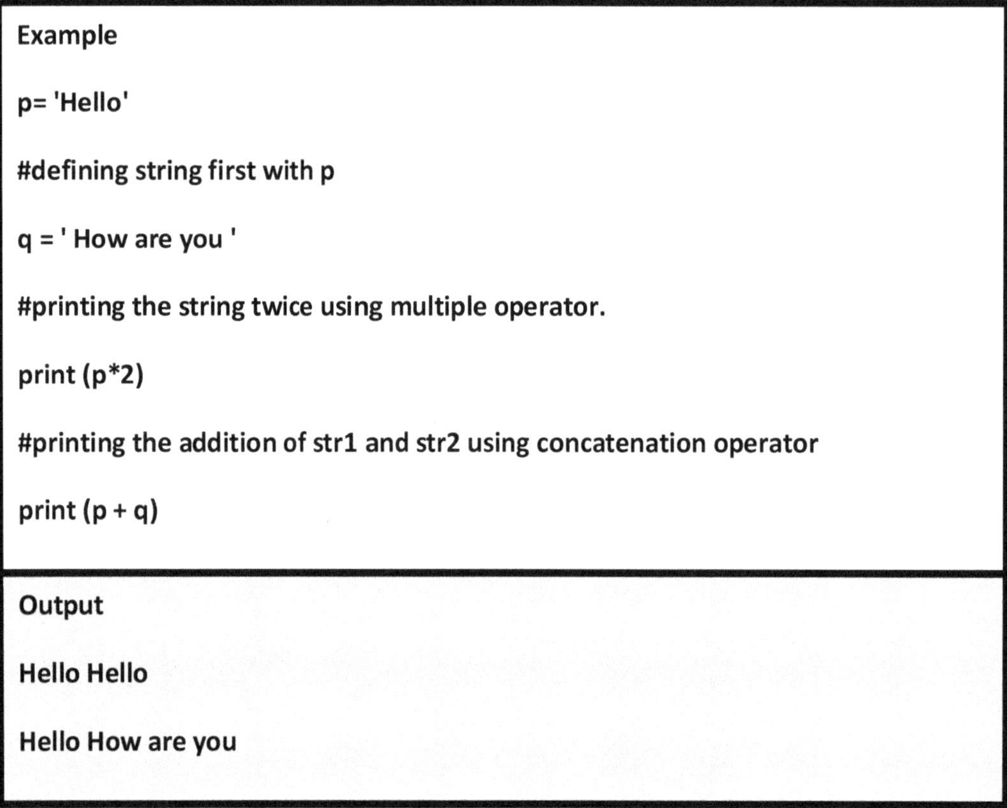

Example

```
p= 'Hello'

#defining string first with p

q = ' How are you '

#printing the string twice using multiple operator.

print (p*2)

#printing the addition of str1 and str2 using concatenation operator

print (p + q)
```

Output

```
Hello Hello

Hello How are you
```

- ✓ In the above code, we have defined two strings, i.e., p and q. Then we used the multiple operators to print string multiple times, and last, we added both strings using + operator.

3.2 List:

- ✓ Lists in Python are similar to arrays present in C, C++, or other programming languages. But unlike arrays, lists in Python can store object values of different data-types.

- ✓ List is an ordered sequence of items. It is one of the most used datatype in Python and is very flexible. All the items in a list do not need to be of the same type.

3.2.1 How to Create Python List:

- ✓ To create python list of items, you need to mention the items, separated by commas, in square brackets. This is the python syntax you need to follow. Then assign it to a variable. Remember once again, you don't need to declare the data type, because Python is dynamically-typed.
- ✓ Declaring a list is pretty straight forward. Items separated by commas are enclosed within brackets [ ].
- ✓ Lists may be constructed in several ways:
- ✓ Using a pair of square brackets to denote the empty list: []

✓ Using a list comprehension: [x for x in iterable]

✓ Using the type constructor: list() or list(iterable)

Syntax-1	Syntax-2	Syntax-3
List name=[]	list name=list()	list name=list(‘string’)

For example, list('abc') returns ['a', 'b', 'c'] and list((1, 2, 3)) returns [1, 2, 3]. If no argument is given, the constructor creates a new empty list, [].

1	>>> colors=['red','green','blue']
2	*A Python list may hold different types of values:* >>> days=['Monday','Tuesday','Wednesday',4,5,6,7.0]

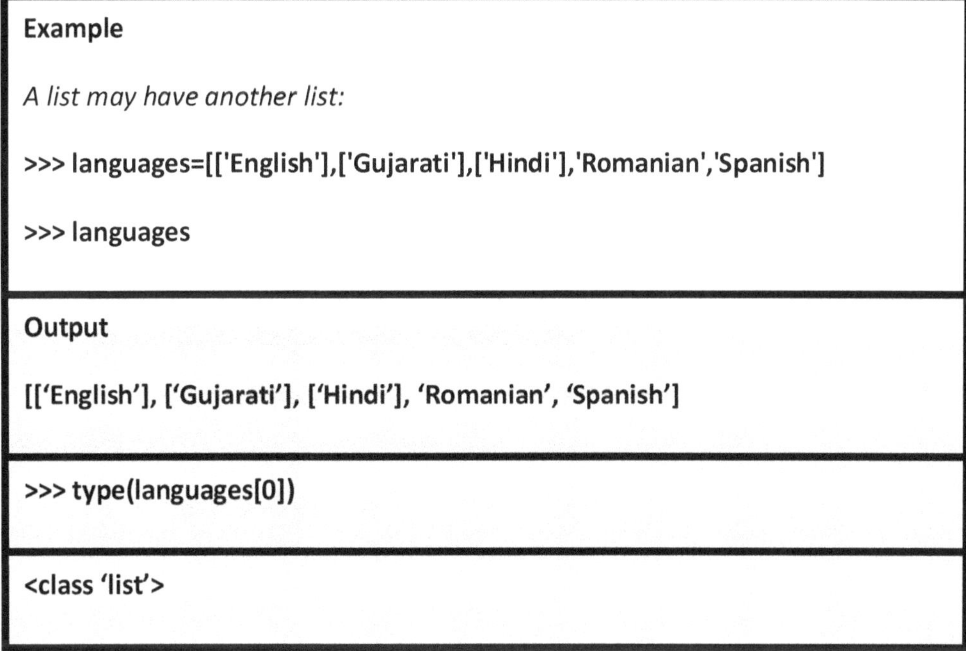

Example
A list may have another list:
>>> languages=[['English'],['Gujarati'],['Hindi'],'Romanian','Spanish']
>>> languages

Output [[‘English’], [‘Gujarati’], [‘Hindi’], ‘Romanian’, ‘Spanish’]
>>> type(languages[0])
<class ‘list’>

3.2.2 How to Access Python List:

✓ To access a Python list as a whole, all you need is its name Or, you can put it in a print statement.

Example	Output
>>> days	['Monday', 'Tuesday', 'Wednesday', 4, 5, 6, 7.0]

- ✓ To access a single element, use its index in square brackets after the list's name. Indexing begins at 0.

3.2.3 Slicing a Python List

- ✓ When you want only a part of a Python list, you can use the slicing operator [].

Example	Output

>>> indices=['zero','one','two','three','four','five']
>>> indices[2:4]
NOTE: This returns items from index 2 to index 4-1 (i.e., 3)
	['two', 'three']

>>> indices[:4] **NOTE:**This returns items from the beginning of the list to index 3.	['zero', 'one', 'two', 'three']
>>> indices[4:] It returns items from index 4 to the end of the list in Python.	['four', 'five']
>>> indices[:] This returns the whole list.	['zero', 'one', 'two', 'three', 'four', 'five']

3.2.4Negative indices: The indices we mention can be negative as well. A negative index means traversal from the end of the list.

Example		Output
>>> indices[:-2]	This returns item from the list's beginning to two items from the end.	['zero', 'one', 'two', 'three']

>>> indices[1:-2]	It returns items from the item at index 1 to two items from the end.	['one', 'two', 'three']
>>> indices[-2:-1]	This returns items from two from the end to one from the end.	['four']
>>> indices[-1:-2]	This returns an empty Python list, because the start is ahead of the stop for the traversal.	[]

3.2.5 Reassigning a Python List (Mutable):

- ✓ Python Lists are mutable. This means that you can reassign its items, or you can reassign it as a whole. Let's take a new list.

>>> colors=['red','green','blue']

(i). Reassigning the whole Python list:

- ✓ You can reassign a Python list by assigning it like a new list.

Example	Output
>>> colors=['yellow','gold','silver','occur'] >>> colors	['yellow', 'gold', 'silver', 'occur']

(ii). Reassigning a few elements

- ✓ You can also reassign a slice of a list in Python.

Example	Output
>>> colors[2:]=['pink','blue']	['yellow', 'gold', 'pink', 'blue']

>>> colors	

(iii). Reassigning a single element

- ✓ You can reassign individual elements too.

Example	Output

>>> colors=['yellow','gold','silver','red']
>>> colors[3]='pink'
>>> colors
	['yellow', 'gold', 'silver', 'pink']

- ✓ Now if you want to add another item 'blue' to the list, we cannot do it the conventional way.
- ✓ So, you need to reassign the whole list for the same.

Example	Output
>>> colors=['yellow','gold','silver','pink','blue'] >>> colors	['yellow', 'gold', 'silver', 'pink','blue']]

3.2.6How can we Delete a Python List:

- ✓ You can delete a Python list, some of its elements, or a single element.

(i). Deleting the entire Python list:

- ✓ Use the del keyword for the same.

Example
>>> del colors
>>> colors
Output
Traceback (most recent call last):File "<pyshell#51>", line 1, in <module>
colors
NameError: name 'colors' is not defined

(ii). Deleting a few elements:

- ✓ Use the slicing operator in python to delete a slice.

Example	Output

>>> colors=['yellow','gold','silver','red','blue']
>>> del colors[2:4]
>>> colors
	['yellow', 'gold', 'blue']

(iii). Deleting a single element:

- ✓ To delete a single element from a Python list, use its index.

Example	Output
>>> del colors[0] >>> colors	['gold', 'blue']

3.2.7Multidimensional Lists in Python:

- ✓ You can also put a list in a list. Let's look at a multidimensional list.

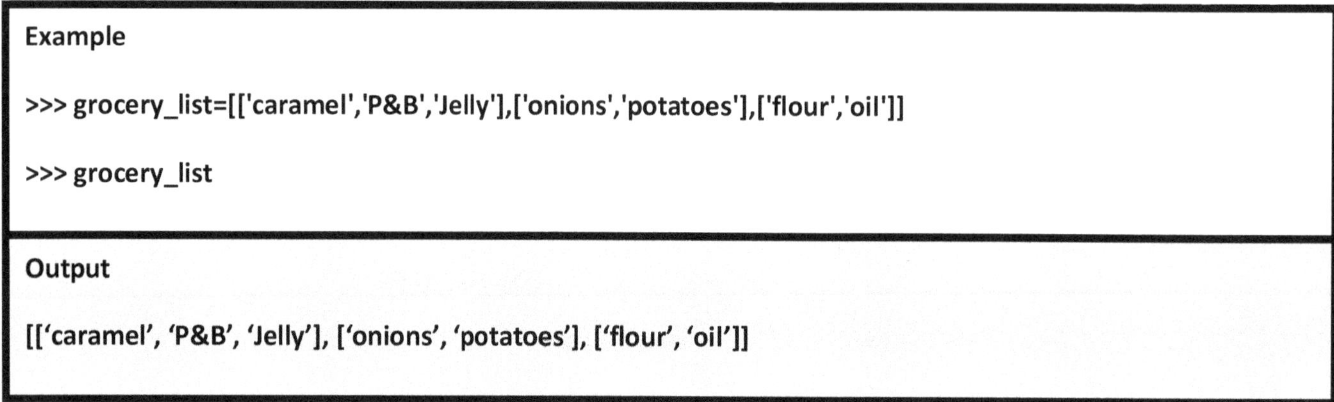

Example
>>> grocery_list=[['caramel','P&B','Jelly'],['onions','potatoes'],['flour','oil']] >>> grocery_list
Output
[['caramel', 'P&B', 'Jelly'], ['onions', 'potatoes'], ['flour', 'oil']]

3.2.8Concatenation of Python List:

- ✓ The concatenation operator works for lists as well. It lets us join two lists, with their orders preserved.

Example	Output
>>> a,b=[3,1,2],[5,4,6] >>> a+b	[3, 1, 2, 5, 4, 6]

3.2.9Python List Operations:

a. Multiplication:

- ✓ This is an arithmetic operation. Multiplying a Python list by an integer makes copies of its items that a number of times while preserving the order.

Example	Output
>>> a*=3 >>> a	[3, 1, 2, 3, 1, 2, 3, 1, 2]

NOTE: However, you can't multiply it by a float.

b. Membership:

- ✓ You can apply the 'in' and 'not in' operators on a Python list.

Example >>> 1 in a	Output True
>>> 2 not in a	False

c.Iterating on a list:

Python list can be traversed with a for loop in python.

Example	Output

>>> for i in [1,2,3]:
    if i%2==0:
        print(f"{i} is composite\n")
	2 is composite

3.2.10Python List Comprehension:

- ✓ You can create a new list just like you would do in mathematics.
- ✓ To do so, type an expression followed by a for statement, all inside square brackets.
- ✓ You may assign it to a variable. Let's make a list for all even numbers from 1 to 20.

Example	Output
>>> even=[2*i for i in range(1,11)] >>> even	[2, 4, 6, 8, 10, 12, 14, 16, 18, 20]

- ✓ Optionally, you can add an if-statement to filter out items.
- ✓ If we want to change this list to hold only those items from 1 to 20 that are even and are divisible by 3, we write the following code.

Example	Output
>>> even=[2*i for i in range(1,11) if i%3==0]	[6, 12, 18]
>>> even	

3.2.11Python List Functions or Built-in Methods:

- ✓ To call a method on a construct, you use the dot-operator(.).
- ✓ Python supports some built-in methods to alter a Python list.

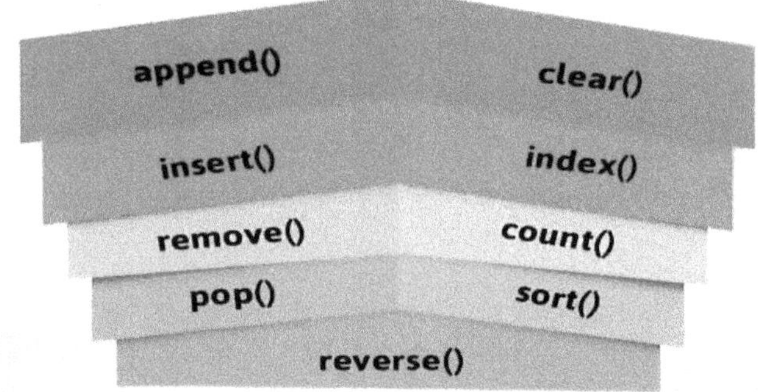

i. **len():** This function returns the length of the list passed as an argument.

ii. **min():** This function returns the minimum element of the list passed as an argument.

iii. **max():** This function returns the maximum element of the list passed as an argument.

Example	Output
ls = [1 , 6 , 7 , 4 , 3]	5
print(len(ls))	1
print(min(ls))	7
print(max(ls))	

iv. **count():** This function returns the number of times an element is present in the list

Example	Output
ls = [34 , 37 , 39 , 24 , 37, 37, 37, 37, 37, 37 , 37 ,37]	**9**
print(ls.count(37))	

v. **remove():** This function is utilized to remove the first occurrence of the specified member from the list

Example	Output
ls = [34 , 37 , 39 , 24 , 37, 37, 37, 37]	[34 , 39 , 24 , 37, 37, 37, 37]
ls.remove(37)	
print(ls)	

✓ Here if we notice carefully, the very first occurrence of 37 is removed from the list

vi. **sort():** This python function is utilized to sort the list passed as an argument in ascending order.

Example	Output
ls = [34 , 37 , 39 , 24 , 86 , 47]	[24, 34 , 37 , 39 , 47 , 86]
ls.sort()	
print(ls)	

vii. **reverse():** This python function is utilized to reverse the list passed as an argument.

Example	Output
ls = [34 , 37 , 39 , 24]	**[24,39,37,34]**
lst.reverse()	
print(ls)	

viii. **clear():** This function is utilized to empty the list passed as an argument to this function.

Example	Output
ls= [34 , 37 , 39 , 24 , 37, 34, 35, 38 , 36 , 33 , 17 , 25, 86 , 47] ls.clear() print(ls)	[]

ix. **append():**It adds an item to the end of the list

Example	Output
>>> a	[2, 1, 3]
>>> a.append(4) >>> a	[2, 1, 3, 4]

x. **insert():**It inserts an item at a specified position.

Example	Output

>>> a.insert(3,5)
>>> a
This inserted the element 5 at index 3.
	[2, 1, 3, 5, 4]

xi. **remove():**It removes the first instance of an item from the Python list.

Example	Output

>>> a=[2,1,3,5,2,4]
>>> a.remove(2)
>>> a
	[1, 3, 5, 2, 4]

xii. **pop():**It removes the element at the specified index, and prints it to the screen.

Example	Output
>>> a.pop(3) >>> a	[1, 3, 5, 4]

xiii. **index():**It returns the first matching index of the item specified.

Example	Output
>>> a=[1,3,5,3,4] >>> a.index(3)	1

xiv. **reverse():**It reverses the order of elements in the Python lists.

Example	Output
>>> a.reverse() >>> a	[5, 4, 3, 3, 1]

3.3 Tuple:

- ✓ Tuple data-type in Python is used to hold multiple object values in a single variable.
- ✓ Tuple data-type is one of the built-in data-type in Python.

3.3.1 Def of Tuple:

- ✓ Tuples are ordered collections of heterogeneous data that are unchangeable. Heterogeneous means tuple can store variables of all types.

3.3.2 Characteristics of Tuple:

- ❖ ***Ordered:*** Tuples are part of sequence data types, which means they hold the order of the data insertion. It maintains the index value for each item.
- ❖ ***Unchangeable:*** Tuples are unchangeable, which means that we cannot add or delete items to the tuple after creation.

- ***Heterogeneous:*** Tuples are a sequence of data of different data types (like integer, float, list, string, etc;) and can be accessed through indexing and slicing.
- ***Contains Duplicates:*** Tuples can contain duplicates, which means they can have items with the same value.

3.3.3 Creating a Tuple:

- ✓ We can create a tuple using the two ways
- ✓ ***Using parenthesis ():*** A tuple is created by enclosing comma-separated items inside rounded brackets.
- ✓ ***Using a tuple() constructor:*** Create a tuple by passing the comma-separated items inside the tuple().
- ✓ A tuple can have items of different data type integer, float, list, string, etc;

Syntax-1	Syntax-2
Tuple name=(list of items)	Tuple name=tuple(list of items)

Example:

Example	Output

# number tuple 	
a= (10, 20, 25.75)
print(a)
	(10, 20, 25.75)

# string tuple 	
b = ('Rishi', 'Shiva', 'uday')
print(b)
	('Rishi', 'Shiva', 'uday')

# mixed type tuple 	
e = ('uday', 30, 45.75, [25, 78])
print(e)
	('uday', 30, 45.75, [25, 78])

# create a tuple using tuple() constructor	('Tarun', 30, 45.75, [23, 78])

d = tuple(('Tarun', 30, 45.75, [23, 78])) print(d)	

- ✓ As we can see in the above output, the different items are added in the tuple like integer, string, and list.

3.3.4 Accessing items of a Tuple:

- ✓ Tuple can be accessed through indexing and slicing. This section will guide you by accessing tuple using the following two ways

  1. Using indexing, we can access any item from a tuple using its index number
  2. Using slicing, we can access a range of items from a tuple

3.3.4.1 Indexing:

- ✓ We can access an item of a tuple by using its index number inside the index operator [] and this process is called "Indexing".

Note: As tuples are ordered sequences of items, the index values start from 0 to the tuple's length.

- ✓ Whenever we try to access an item with an index more than the tuple's length, it will throw the 'Index Error'.
- ✓ Similarly, the index values are always integer. If we give any other type, then it will throw Type Error.

(i)Python positive and negative indexing:

- ✓ In the above image, we can see that the index values start from zero and it goes till the last item whose index value will be len(tuple) - 1 .

Example	Output
uday = ('P', 'Y', 'T', 'H', 'O', 'N') for i in range(4): print(uday[i])	P Y T H

- ✓ As seen in the above example, we print the tuple's first four items with the indexing.

Note: If we mention the index value greater than the length of a tuple then it will throw an index error.

(ii) Negative Indexing:

- ✓ The index values can also be negative, with the last but the first items having the index value as -1 and second last -2 and so on.
- ✓ For example, We can access the last item of a tuple using tuple_name[-1].
- ✓ Access tuple items using the negative index value.Iterate tuple using negative indexing

Example	Output
# iterate a tuple using negative indexing for i in range(-6, 0): print(uday[i], end=", ")	P, Y, T, H, O, N,

3.3.5 Slicing a tuple:

- ✓ We can even specify a range of items to be accessed from a tuple using the technique called 'Slicing.' The operator used is ':'.
- ✓ We can specify the start and end values for the range of items to be accessed from the tuple.
- ✓ The output will be a tuple, and it includes the range of items with the index values from the start till the end of the range.
- ✓ The end value item will be excluded.

Example	Output
h = (0, 1, 2, 3, 4, 5, 6, 7, 8, 9, 10) print(h[1:5])	(1, 2, 3, 4)
print(h[:5])	(0, 1, 2, 3, 4)
print(h[6:])	(6, 7, 8, 9, 10)

3.3.6 Packing and Unpacking

- ✓ A tuple can also be created without using a tuple() constructor or enclosing the items inside the parentheses. It is called the variable "Packing."

- ✓ In Python, we can create a tuple by packing a group of variables. Packing can be used when we want to collect multiple values in a single variable. Generally, this operation is referred to as tuple packing.
- ✓ Similarly, we can unpack the items by just assigning the tuple items to the same number of variables. This process is called "Unpacking."
- ✓ Let us see this with an example.

Example	Output

# packing variables into tuple 	
sai = 1, 2, "Hello"
# display tuple 	
print(sai)
	(1, 2, 'Hello')

print(type(sai))	class 'tuple'

# unpacking tuple into variable 	
i, j, k = sai
# printing the variables 	
print(i, j, k)
	1 2 Hello

- ✓ As we can see in the above output, three tuple items are assigned to individual variables i, j, k, respectively.
- ✓ In case we assign fewer variables than the number of items in the tuple, we will get the value error with the message too many values to unpack

3.3.7 Adding and changing items in a Tuple

- ✓ A list is a mutable type, which means we can add or modify values in it, but tuples are immutable, so they cannot be changed.
- ✓ Also, because a tuple is immutable there are no built-in methods to add items to the tuple.
- ✓ If you try to modify the value you will get an error.

Example charan = (0, 1, 2, 3, 4, 5) charan[1] = 10
Output TypeError: 'tuple' object does not support item assignment

- ✓ As the solution is , we can convert the tuple to a list, add items, and then convert it back to a tuple. As tuples are ordered collection like lists the items always get added in the end.

Example	Output
sai = (0, 1, 2, 3, 4, 5) # converting tuple into a list ls= list(sai) # add item to list ls.append(6) # converting list back into a tuple q = tuple(ls) print(q)	(0, 1, 2, 3, 4, 5, 6)

3.3.8 Removing items from a tuple

- ✓ Tuples are immutable so there are no pop() or remove() methods for the tuple. We can remove the items from a tuple using the following two ways.

  i. ***Using del keyword***

  ii. ***By converting it into a list***

i.Using del keyword:

- ✓ The del keyword will delete the entire tuple.

Example	**Output**
sai =(0,1,2,3,4,5,6,7,8,9,10) **del sai** **print(sai)**	**NameError: name 'sampletup1' is not defined**

- ✓ As seen in the above output we are getting error when we try to access a deleted tuple.

ii.By converting it into a List:

- ✓ We can convert a tuple into a list and then remove any one item using the remove() method.
- ✓ Then again we will convert it back into a tuple using the tuple() constructor.

Example	**Output**
t = (0, 1, 2, 3, 4, 5) **# converting tuple into a list** **s = list(t)** **# reomve 2nd item** **s.remove(2)** **# converting list back into a tuple** **p = tuple(s)** **print(p)**	**(0, 1, 3, 4, 5)**

- ✓ As seen in the above output item 3 has been removed from the tuple.

3.3.9 Differences between Tuples and Lists

	List	Tuple
Syntax	List is represented with square brackets []	Tuple is represented with parentheses ()
Mutable/Immutable	List is mutable object	Tuple is immutable object
Built-in methods	List supports many built-in methods such as insert, pop, remove, etc.	Tuple doesn't support as many built-in methods as list
Storage/memory Efficiency	List consumes a lot of memory/storage	Tuple consumes a lot less storage/memory
Time Efficiency	Creation of list and accessing the list elements is slower	Creation of tuple and accessing the tuple elements is faster

3.4 Dictionary Data-type:

- ✓ The dictionary data-type in Python is a set of key-value pairs of items in an unordered manner.
- ✓ Keys in a dictionary can only hold primitive data-types, whereas the object values are arbitrary objects in Python.
- ✓ In the dictionary, items are closed inside in the curly braces {}
- ✓ In the dictionary, items are separated from each other through a comma ().

3. 4.1 How Do You Create a Dictionary in Python

- ✓ You create a Python dictionary using curly brackets or the "dict" function. You can either pre-fill the dictionary upon creation or add items after the dictionary has been initialized.
- ✓ Creating a dictionary is as simple as placing items inside curly braces {} separated by commas.
- ✓ An item has a key and a corresponding value that is expressed as a pair (key: value).
- ✓ While the values can be of any data type and can repeat, keys must be of immutable type (string, number or tuple with immutable elements) and must be unique.

Syntax-1	Syntax-2

#Creating an empty dictionary
dictionary = {}
	#Creating an empty dictionary with the dict function
	dictionary = dict()

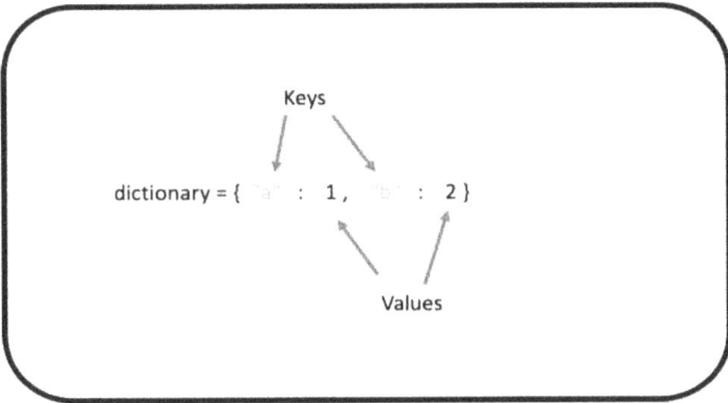

3.4.2 Initializing a dictionary with values:

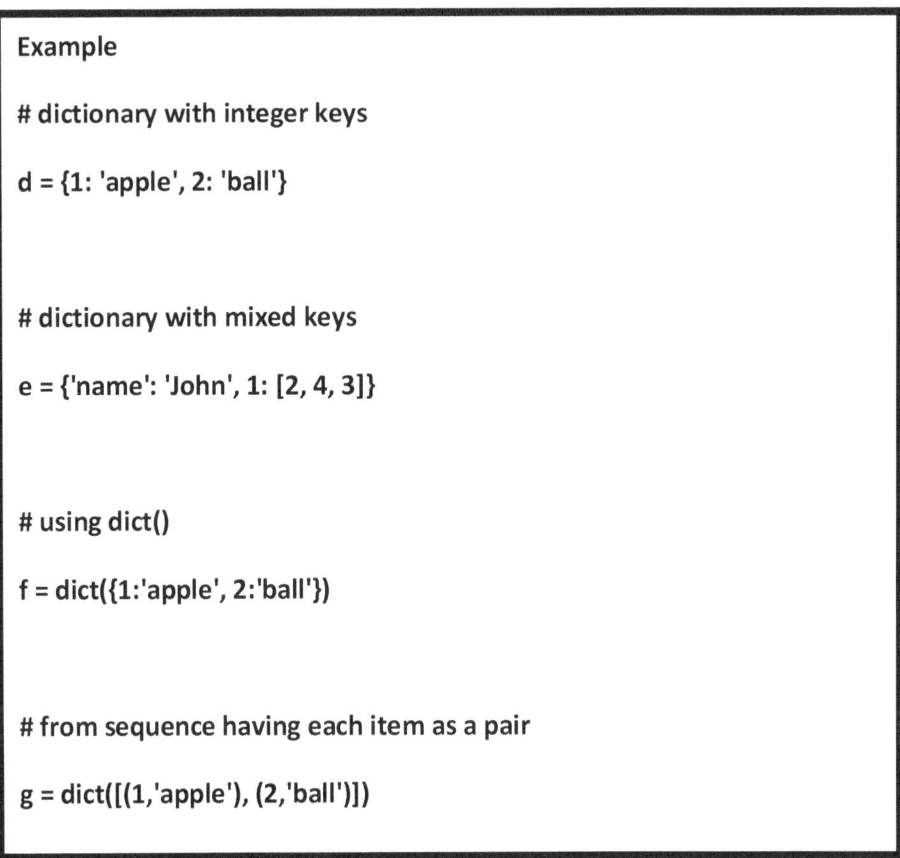

Example

```
# dictionary with integer keys
d = {1: 'apple', 2: 'ball'}


# dictionary with mixed keys
e = {'name': 'John', 1: [2, 4, 3]}


# using dict()
f = dict({1:'apple', 2:'ball'})


# from sequence having each item as a pair
g = dict([(1,'apple'), (2,'ball')])
```

3.4.3 How to Add values to Dictionary:

- ✓ You add values to a dictionary by indexing a new key and assigning a value to it.

Example	Output
d = {} d["c"] = 3 print(d)	{'c': 3}

3.4.4 How to Sort a Dictionary in Python:

- ✓ The purpose of a dictionary is to find specific values by their respective keys. Accordingly, the order of items in a dictionary shouldn't matter in most cases.

(i)Sort a Dictionary by Value

- ✓ If you do want to order a dictionary alphabetically or numerically by its values, you can do so by retrieving the values and applying the sorted function.

Example	Output
d = {"c": 3, "a" : 1, "d" : 4, "b" : 2} sorted(d.values())	[1, 2, 3, 4]

- ✓ The result is a list of values without the keys. But you shouldn't need the keys anyways, because their only job in a dictionary is to provide a mapping to the values.
- ✓ If the values follow an order by which they can be found, the keys become obsolete.

(ii)Sort a Dictionary by Key

- ✓ To order a dictionary by its keys, you can use a combination of the sorted function and a lambda expression.

Example	Output
d = {"c": 3, "a" : 1, "d" : 4, "b" : 2} temp= sorted(d.items(), key=lambda x: x[1]) print(temp)	[('a', 1), ('b', 2), ('c', 3), ('d', 4)]

Example:

Example	Output
d = {1:'sai', 2:'ram', 3:'ravi', 4:'siva'}	**{1:'sai', 2:'ram', 3:'ravi', 4:'siva'}**
print (d)	**1st name is sai**
print("1st name is "+d[1])	**2nd name is ram**
print("2nd name is "+ d[2])	**dict_keys([1, 2, 3, 4])**
print (d.keys())	**dict_values(['Jim', 'Carry', 'Jonas', 'Mike'])**
print (d.values())	

Method	Description	Syntax
copy()	Entire dictionary will be copied into a new dictionary	dict.copy()
update()	Helps to update an existing dictionary item	dict.update(dict2)
items()	Used for displaying the items of a dictionary	dict.items()
sort()	allows sorting the dictionary items	dict.sort()
len()	used to determine the total number of items in the dictionary	len(dict)
Str()	Make a dictionary into a printable string format	Str(dict)

3.5 Set data-type:

✓ Set data-type in Python is an unordered collection of data.

✓ The variables with set data-type stores values un-orderly and doesn't have key values.

✓ Since the order of the values is undefined in the set, Python may return the changed sequence of the elements in the set while printing the set in output.

- ✓ Sets are iterable in nature.
- ✓ Sets are also mutable, i.e., we can modify elements of the set after creation.
- ✓ Set always has unique elements stored in them. It doesn't allow duplicity of elements.
- ✓ In Python, a set can contain various types of values with different data-types.

3.5.1 Defining a set in Python:

- ✓ In Python, we can define the set using the following two methods:

a)*We can create a set variable in our Python program using Python's built-in set () function.*

b)*We can pass sequence of elements inside the curly braces {} and separate the values by comma {,}.*

Example	Output

# Creating a set(P) using built-in set() function in Python 	
P = set()
# the P is an empty set 	
# creating a set(Q) by passing sequence elements in curly braces 	
Q = {'Niyansh', 2, 3,'Python'}
# Check the class type of P and Q 	
print(type(P))
print(type(Q))
# Printing the values present in Q 	
print(Q)
	<class 'set'>
	<class 'set'>
	{Niyansh', 2, 3,'Python'}

Explanation: In the above code, we have defined two sets i.e. P and Q.

The P is empty set whereas Q is storing some elements.

3.6 Boolean data-type:

- ✓ Like any other programming language in Python, boolean data-type has two built-in values, i.e., true and false.
- ✓ Boolean data-type is used for the condition statement codes to check if the statement is true or false.

- ✓ The class bool denotes the boolean data-type.
- ✓ True in boolean data-type can be represented by any non-zero value or 'T'.
- ✓ False in boolean data-type can be represented by zero value (0) or 'F'.
- ✓ Example: Look at the following code for boolean type:

Example	Output
# A Python program to check the boolean data-type **print(type(False))** **print(type(True))** **print(true)**	**<class 'bool'>** **<class 'bool'>** **NameError: name 'true' is not defined**

- ✓ We can see that the true or false value (with quotation marks) will be treated as Boolean type, and they are used for conditional statements.
- ✓ We will discuss Boolean type, and it's working in Python in detail later tutorial.

You can enter the text of the second chapter here.

The headers used in Body text are 'Book title' on the left-side page and 'Author name' or 'Chapter name' on the right-side page. Pages in which chapters start would not have headers or footers.

You can also insert images inside the book. We've provided a sample here.

If you wish to print the images in color, be sure to insert color images with atleast a resolution of 300 dpi and choose the full-color option when you set up the book on the platform. Also, please note that making the book full-color would substantially increase the printing cost and, therefore, the MRP of the book.

3. Functions

1.Function:

- ✓ In Python, a function is a group of related statements that performs a specific task.
- ✓ A function can be defined as the organized block of reusable code, which can be called whenever required.
- ✓ Functions help break our program into smaller and modular chunks. As our program grows larger and larger, functions make it more organized and manageable.
- ✓ Furthermore, it avoids repetition and makes the code reusable.
- ✓ Reusability:- once we are writing function means, we can call any number of times.
- ✓ Easy Debugging means finding errors are easier.
- ✓ A function is a block of code which only runs when it is called.
- ✓ You can pass data, known as parameters, into a function.
- ✓ A function can return data as a result.
- ✓ You can pass data, known as parameters, into a function.
- ✓ A function can return data as a result.

1.1 Types of functions:

Note: In other languages functions are known as methods, procedures and subroutines etc

Python supports 2 types of functions

i. Built in Functions

ii. User Defined Functions

1.1.1 Built in Functions:

The functions which are coming along with Python software automatically, are called built in functions or pre defined functions

Ex:-

- ✓ id()
- ✓ type()
- ✓ input()
- ✓ eval()

1.1.2 User Defined Functions:

- ✓ The functions which are developed by programmer explicitly according to business requirements, are called user defined functions.
- ✓ Function definition must consists of the following components.
    1. Every function should start with "def" keyword
    2. Every function should have name (not equal to any keyword)

Syntax-1	Syntax-2
deffun_name(with or without parameters): statement(s)	deffun_name(parameters): function_block return expression

- ✓ Keyword def that marks the start of the function header.
- ✓ A function name to uniquely identify the function. Function naming follows the same rules of writing identifiers in Python.
- ✓ Parameters (arguments) through which we pass values to a function. They are optional.
- ✓ A colon (:) to mark the end of the function header.
- ✓ One or more valid python statements that make up the function body. Statements must have the same indentation level.
- ✓ An optional return statement to return a value from the function.

Example-1

```
defmy_function():
    print("Hello from a function")
```

1.2 Calling a Function:

- ✓ To call a function, use the function name followed by parenthesis:
- ✓ Once we have defined a function, we can call it from another function, program, or even the Python prompt. To call a function we simply type the function name with appropriate parameters.
- ✓ To execute a function it needs to be called. This is called function calling.
- ✓ Function name

- ✓ Argument/parameter

Syntax
Function name(parameters)

- ✓ Note: In python, the function definition should always be present before the function call. Otherwise, we will get an error.
- ✓ In Python, after the function is created, we can call it from another function.
- ✓ A function must be defined before the function call; otherwise, the Python interpreter gives an error.
- ✓ To call the function, use the function name followed by the parentheses.
- ✓ Consider the following example of a simple example that prints the message "Hello World".

<table>
<tr><th>Example</th><th>Output</th></tr>
<tr><td>defmy_function():
    print("Hello ")
my_function()</td><td>Hello</td></tr>
</table>

<table>
<tr><th>Example</th><th>Output</th></tr>
<tr><td>def wish():
    print("Hello Good Morning")
wish()
wish()
wish()</td><td>Hello Good Morning
Hello Good Morning
Hello Good Morning</td></tr>
<tr><td>def sum(x,y):
    s=x+y
print("sum of two numbers:",s)
sum(10,20)
sum(30,60)</td><td>sum of two numbers: 30
sum of two numbers: 90</td></tr>
</table>

- ✓ Parameters (arguments) through which we pass values to a function. They are optional and these are included in between parenthesis.

- ✓ Every function with/without argument should end with(:)
- ✓ One or more valid python statements that make up the function body. Statements must have the same indentation level (usually 4 spaces).
- ✓ An optional return statement to return a value from the function.

Note: While creating functions we can use 2 keywords

- ✓ def (mandatory)
- ✓ return (optional)

1.3 Arguments:

- ✓ The terms parameter and argument can be used for the same thing: information that are
- ✓ passed into a function.
- ✓ From a function's perspective:
- ✓ A parameter is the variable listed inside the parentheses in the function definition.
- ✓ An argument is the value that is sent to the function when it is called.
- ✓ Information can be passed into functions as arguments.
- ✓ Arguments are specified after the function name, inside the parentheses. You can add as many arguments as you want, just separate them with a comma.
- ✓ The following example has a function with one argument (fname). When the function is called, we pass along a first name, which is used inside the function to print the full name.

Example	**Output**
defmyfunction(fname): print(fname + " is good") myfunction("rosy") myfunction("lily") myfunction("krish")	Rosy is good Lily is good Krish is good

Types of Arguments in Python:

There are 4 types are actual arguments are allowed in Python.

i. positional arguments (Required arguments)
ii. keyword arguments (named arguments)
iii. default arguments
iv. Variable length arguments

1.3.1 positional arguments (Required arguments):

These are the arguments passed to function in correct positional order.

Example

```
def sub(a,b):
    print(a-b)

sub(100,200)
sub(200,100)
sub(200) #error
```

- ✓ When the function call statement encountered must match the number and order of arguments as defined in the function definition. It is positional argument matching.
- ✓ The number of arguments and position of arguments must be matched. If we change the order then result may be changed.
- ✓ If we change the number of arguments then we will get error.

Example	Output

def sum(a,b):
    c=a+b
    print(c)
 	
sum(10,20)
sum(20)
	30
	Error

1.3.2 keyword arguments (named arguments):

- ✓ We can pass argument values by keyword i.e by parameter name.
- ✓ Using the keyword argument, the argument passed in function call is matched with function definition on the basis of the name of parameter.

Example	Output
defmsg(id,name): print(id)	100 sri

print(name) msg(id=100,name="sri") msg(name="sai",id=200)	200 Sai

Example	Output
def wish(name,msg): print("Hello",name,msg) wish(name="sri",msg="Good Morning") wish(msg="Good Morning",name="sri")	Hello sri Good Morning Hello sri Good Morning

- ✓ Here the order of arguments is not important but number of arguments must be matched.

Note:

We can use both positional and keyword arguments simultaneously. But first we have to take positional arguments and then keyword arguments, otherwise we will get syntax error.

Example

```
def wish(name,msg):
        print("Hello",name,msg)
wish("sir", "GoodMorning") ==>valid
wish("sir", msg="GoodMorning") ==>valid
wish(name="sir", "GoodMorning") ==>invalid
```

Syntax Error: positional argument follows keyword argument

1.3.3 Default Argument:

- ✓ If we call the function without argument, it uses the default value.

Example	Output

def fun(country = "Norway"): print("I am from " + country)fun("Sweden") fun("India") fun() fun("Brazil")	I am from Sweden I am from India I am from Norway I am from Brazil

Note:

After default arguments we should not take non default arguments

- ✓ def wish(name="Guest",msg="Good Morning"): =====>Valid
- ✓ def wish(name,msg="Good Morning"): ===========>Valid
- ✓ def wish(name="Guest",msg): ==================>Invalid

SyntaxError: non-default argument follows default argument

1.3.4 Variable-length arguments:

Example	**Output**

def my(*kids):
for i in range(0,len(kids)):
print(kids[i])
my("sri","sai","ram")
	sri
	sai
	ram

- ✓ If you do not know how many arguments that will be passed into your function, add a * before the parameter name in the function definition.
- ✓ This way the function will receive a tuple of arguments, and can access the items accordingly:

Note:

- ✓ Parameters to functions are references to objects, which are passed by value. When you pass a variable to a function, python passes the reference to the object to which the variable refers (the value). Not the variable itself.
- ✓ Python supports pass by reference rather than pass by value due to its constraints.
- ✓ All parameters (arguments) in the Python language are passed by reference. It means if you change what a parameter refers to within a function, the change also reflects back in the calling function.

Example

```
def change(mylist):
mylist.append([1,2,3,4])
        print("inside function:", mylist)
        return
mylist=[10,20,30]
change(mylist)
print("outside function:", mylist)
```

Output

```
inside function: [10, 20, 30, [1, 2, 3, 4]]
outside function: [10, 20, 30, [1, 2, 3, 4]]
```

Note:

Here, we are maintaining reference of the passed object and appending values in the same object. So, this would produce the following result

Example

```
def swap(a,b):
        t=a
        a=b
        b=t
        print("after swap inside function:", a,b)
        return a,b
a=int(input("enter a:"))
b=int(input("enter b:"))
a,b=swap(a,b)
print("swap outside function:", a,b)
```

Output

```
enter a:3
enter b:4
```

after swap inside function: 4 3 swap outside function: 4 3

1.4 Return Statement:

Function can take input values as parameters and executes business logic, and returns output to the caller with return statement.

Example	**Output**
def add(x, y): return x+y result=add(10,20) print("The sum is",result) print("The sum is",add(100,200))	The sum is 30 The sum is 300

1.4.1 Returning multiple values from a function:

In other languages like C,C++ and Java, function can return at most one value. But in Python, a function can return any number of values.

Example	**Output**

defsum_sub(x,y):
        sum=x+y
        sub=x-y
return sum,sub
r1,r2=sum_sub(12,3)
print("result r1:", r1)
print("result r2:", r2)
	result r1: 15
	result r2: 9

defallop(x,y):
        sum=x+y
        sub=x-y
mul=x*y
        div=x/y
return sum,sub,mul,div
	127
	121
	372
	41.333333333333336

res=allop(124,3) for i in res: print(i)	

2.Recursion:

- ✓ Recursion is the process of defining something in terms of itself.
- ✓ In Python, we know that a function can call other functions. It is even possible for the function to call itself. These types of construct are termed as recursive functions.

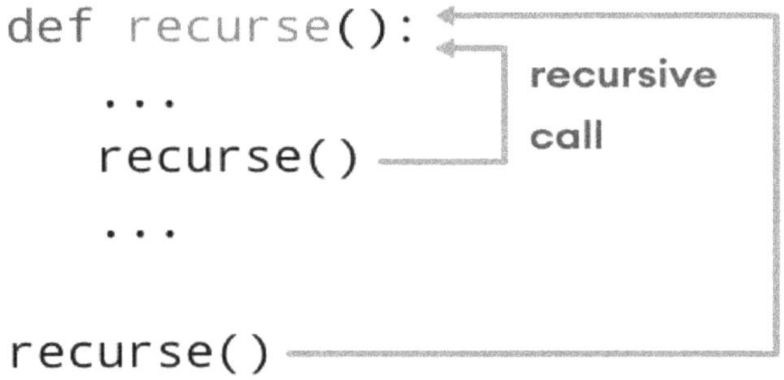

```
def recurse():
    ...
    recurse()
    ...

recurse()
```

recursive call

Example	Output

#program to calculate factorial of given number
def fact(n):
    if(n==1):
        return 1
    else:
        return n*fact(n-1)
 	
n=int(input("enter a number:"))
res=fact(n)
print("factorial of ", n,"is",res)
	enter a number:5
	factorial of 5 is 120

Example	Output

# program to find the sum of natural numbers 	
def sum(n):
    if n <= 1:
        return n
    else:
        return n + sum(n-1)
num = 16
if num< 0:
  print("Enter a positive number")
else:
  print("The sum is“, sum(num))
	The sum is 136

Example	Output

# program to find the GCD of 2-numbers 	
defgcd(a,b):
  if(b==0):
    return a
  else:
    return gcd(b,a%b)
a=int(input("Enter first number:"))
b=int(input("Enter second number:"))
res=gcd(a,b)
print("Result is: “,res)
	Enter first number:5
	Enter second number:15
	Result is: 5

3.Files in Python

- ✓ Files are named locations on disk to store related information. They are used to permanently store data in a non-volatile memory (e.g. hard disk).
- ✓ When we want to read from or write to a file, we need to open it first.
- ✓ When we are done, it needs to be closed so that the resources that are tied with the file are freed.
- ✓ Hence, in Python, a file operation takes place in the following order:

i. Open a file
ii. Read or write (perform operation)
iii. Close the file

3.1 Opening Files in Python:

- ✓ Python provides an open() function that accepts two arguments, file name and access mode in which the file is accessed.
- ✓ The function returns a file object which can be used to perform various operations like reading, writing, etc

Syntax file object = open("file-name", "access-mode")
Example f= open("demofile.txt", "r")

Accessing Modes of File:

- ✓ We can specify the mode while opening a file. The files can be accessed using various modes:
- ✓ "r" - **Read** - Default value. Opens a file for reading, error if the file does not exist
- ✓ "a" - **Append** - Opens a file for appending, creates the file if it does not exist
- ✓ "w" - **Write** - Opens a file for writing, creates the file if it does not exist
- ✓ "x" - **Create** - Creates the specified file, returns an error if the file exists.
- ✓ "t"-**Text**-Opens in text mode. (default)
- ✓ "b"-**Binary**-Opens in binary mode.
- ✓ "+" Opens a file for updating (reading and writing)

Note:

- ✓ To open a file for reading it is enough to specify the name of the file:

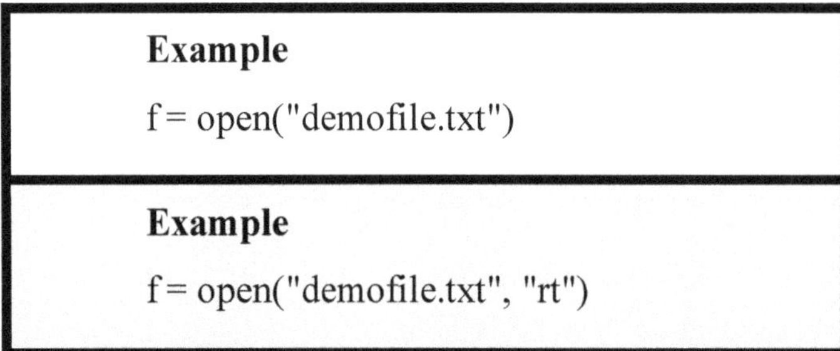

Example f= open("demofile.txt")
Example f= open("demofile.txt", "rt")

- ✓ Because "r" for read, and "t" for text are the default values, you do not need to specify them.

3.2 Closing Files in Python:

- ✓ When we are done with performing operations on the file, we need to properly close the file.
- ✓ The syntax to use the **close()** method is given below.

Syntax
fileobject.close()

- ✓ After closing the file, we cannot perform any operation in the file.

3.3 Perform Read operation or write operation:

(i)Writing the file:

- ✓ In order to write into a file in Python, we need to open it in write" w", append "a" or exclusive creation "x "mode.
- ✓ We need to be careful with the w mode, as it will overwrite into the file if it already exists. Due to this, all the previous data are erased.
- ✓ Writing a string or sequence of bytes (for binary files) is done using the write() method. This method returns the number of characters written to the file.

Syntax

fileobject.write("------------------")

Example

```
f=open("test.txt",'w')
f.write("my first file\n")
f.write("This file\n\n")
f.write("contains three lines\n")
f.close()
```

(ii) Reading the Files:

- ✓ To read a file in Python, we must open the file in reading r mode.
- ✓ There are various methods available for this purpose:

-read()

-read(size)

-readline()

-readlines()

- Read file through for loop

- **read() :**
  - ✓ By default the read() method returns the whole text.

Syntax fileobject.read()
Example f= open("demofile.txt", "r") print(f.read())

- **read(size):**
  - ✓ you can also specify how many characters you want to return
  - ✓ The read(size) method returns the specified no of characters.

Syntax fileobject.read(size)
Example f= open("demofile.txt", "r") print(f.read(5))

  - ✓ The above code will return the 5 first characters of the file.

- **readline():**
  - ✓ The readline() method reads the lines of the file from the beginning, i.e., if we use the readline() method two times, then we can get the first two lines of the file.

Syntax fileobject.readline()

Example

```
f= open("file2.txt","r");
l1 = f.readline()
l2 = f.readline()
print(l1)
print(l2)
f.close()
```

Note: We called the readline() function two times that's why it read two lines from the file.

- **readlines():**
  - ✓ Python also provides the readlines() method which is used for the reading lines.
  - ✓ It will returns a list which contains all the lines of the entire file.

Syntax

```
fileobject.readlines()
```

Example

```
f= open("file2.txt","r");
res = f.readlines()
print(res)
f.close()
```

- **Read file through for loop:**
  - ✓ We can read the file using for loop.

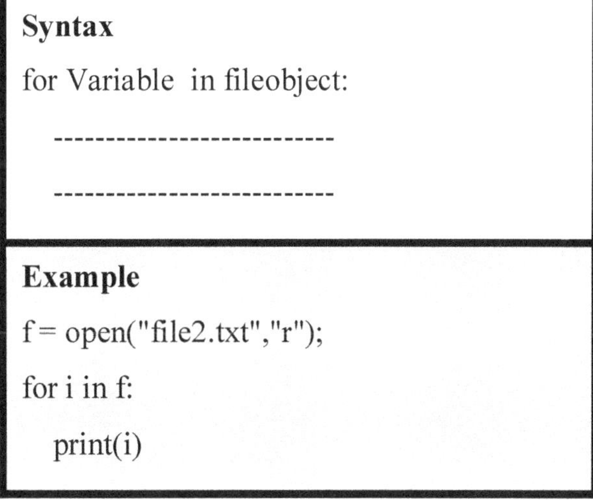

Syntax

```
for Variable  in fileobject:
    ---------------------------
    ---------------------------
```

Example

```
f= open("file2.txt","r");
for i in f:
    print(i)
```

❖ **The with statement**

- ✓ The with statement was introduced in python 2.5.
- ✓ The with statement is useful in the case of manipulating the files.
- ✓ It is used in the scenario where a pair of statements is to be executed with a block of code in between.
- ✓ The syntax to open a file using with the statement is :

Syntax

```
with open("file name", "access mode") as fileobject:
    #statement suite
```

Example

```
with open("file.txt",'r') as f:
    res = f.read();
    print(res)
```

Example

```
with open ("file.txt", "w") as f:
f.write ("Hello World!!!")
```

- ✓ The advantage of using with statement is that it provides the guarantee to close the file regardless of how the nested block exits.
- ✓ It is always suggestible to use the with statement in the case of files because, if the break, return, or exception occurs in the nested block of code then it automatically closes the file,
- ✓ we don't need to write the close() function. It doesn't let the file to corrupt.

❖ **split() using file handling**

- ✓ We can also split lines using file handling in Python.
- ✓ This splits the variable when space is encountered.
- ✓ You can also split using any characters as we wish.

Example

```
with open("file.text", "r") as file:
    data = file.readlines()
    for line in data:
        word = line.split()
        print (word)
```

Other Programs:

Example-1

```
#6.a)Program to Read a file line by line into a list
f= open("abc.txt","w")
f.write("iam a student\n")
f.write("studing in aitam college\n")
f.write("which is located in tekkali\n")
f.close()
f2 = open("sai.txt","r")
print(f2.readlines())
```

```
import os
import time
from pathlib import Path
fname=input("enter the path of the file:")
print("file name:",Path(fname).stem)
print("file extension:",Path(fname).suffix)
print("Last modified: %s" % time.ctime(os.path.getmtime(filename)))
print("Created: %s" % time.ctime(os.path.getctime(filename)))
file=open(fname,"r")
count=0
content=file.read()
```

```
clist=content.split("\n")
for line in clist:
    if line:
        count+=1
print("line count:",count)
```

```
#6.c) Reads and displays the content of the file
f2 = open("sai.txt","r")
print(f2.read())
```

#6.d) Write a program that inputs a text file. The program should print all of the unique words in the file in alphabetical order.

```
f= open("abc.txt","r")
l1 = f.readlines()
l2 = []
l3 = []
for i in l1:
    l2.extend(i.split())
for i in lst2:
    if i not in lst3:
        l3.append(i)
l3.sort()
print(l3)
```

4. Modules

1. Namespaces:

- ✓ Python namespaces, the structures used to organize the symbolic names assigned to objects in a Python program.
- ✓ A namespace is a collection of names.
- ✓ A namespace is a way of providing the unique name for each object in Python. Everything in Python is an object, i.e., a variable or a method.
- ✓ An assignment statement creates a symbolic name that you can use to reference an object. The statement s***ai*= *'str'*** creates a symbolic name ***sai*** that refers to the string object ***'str'.***
- ✓ In a program of any complexity, you'll create hundreds or thousands of such names, each pointing to a specific object. How does Python keep track of all these names so that they don't interfere with one another?
- ✓ We are going to study:
    - How Python organizes symbolic names and objects in namespaces
    - When Python creates a new namespace
    - How namespaces are implemented
- ✓ A namespace is a ***collection of currently defined symbolic names*** along with information about the object that each name references.
- ✓ A namespace as a dictionary in which the keys are the object names and the values are the objects themselves.
- ✓ Each key-value pair maps a name to its corresponding object. In a Python program, there are four types of namespaces:
    - ***i. Built-In Namespace***
    - ***ii. Global Namespace***
    - ***iii. Enclosing Namespace***
    - ***iv. Local Namespace***
- ✓ These have differing lifetimes. As Python executes a program, it creates namespaces as necessary and deletes them when they're no longer needed.

i. The Built-In Namespace:

- ✓ The built-in namespace contains the names of all of Python's built-in objects. These are available at all times when Python is running.
- ✓ You can list the objects in the built-in namespace with the following command:

Syntax

```
>>> dir(_builtins_)
```

- ✓ The Python interpreter creates the built-in namespace when it starts up.
- ✓ This namespace remains in existence until the interpreter terminates.

ii. Global Namespace:

- ✓ The global namespace contains any names defined at the level of the main program.
- ✓ Python creates the global namespace when the main program body starts, and it remains in existence until the interpreter terminates.
- ✓ Strictly speaking, this may not be the only one global namespace.
- ✓ The interpreter also creates a global namespace for any module that your program loads with the import statement.

iii. Local and Enclosing Namespaces:

- ✓ The interpreter creates a new namespace whenever a function executes. That namespace is local to the function and remains in existence until the function terminates.

```
def aitam():
    print('I am aitam')

    def eee():
        print('I am eee')
        return

    eee()
    print('I am going from aitam')
    return
aitam()
```

- ✓ In the above example, the function eee() is defined within the body of aitam().

- ✓ Inside the aitam() we called the eee().
- ✓ Let's understand the working of the above function –
- ✓ When we calls aitam(), Python creates a new namespace for aitam().
- ✓ Similarly, the aitam() calls eee(), eee() gets its own separate namespace.
- ✓ Here the eee() is a local namespace created for aitam() is the ***enclosing namespace***.
- ✓ Each of these namespace is terminated when the function is terminated.

2. Modules in Python:

- ✓ Modules are simply files with the ".py" extension containing Python code that can be imported inside another Python Program.
- ✓ Modules refer to a file containing Python statements and definitions.
- ✓ A file containing Python code, for example: ***sai.py***, is called a module, and its module name would be ***sai***.

2.1 How to create modules in python:

- ✓ To create a module, we have to save the code that we wish in a file with the file extension ".py". Then, the name of the Python file becomes the name of the module.
- ✓ Modules in Python provides us the flexibility to organize the code in a logical way.
- ✓ To use the functionality of one module into another, we must have to import the specific module.

Example

- ✓ In this example, we will create a module named as ***eee.py*** which contains a function ***display( )*** that contains a code to print some message on the screen.

```
eee.py
def display(name):
        print("Hi "+name)
```

2.2 How to use Python Modules:

- ✓ We need to load the module in another python code to use its functionality.
- ✓ Python provides two types of statements as defined below.

i. The import statement

ii. The from-import statement

i.The import statement:

- ✓ The import statement is used to import all the functionality of one module into another.
- ✓ Here, we must notice that we can use the functionality of any python source file by importing that file as the module into another python source file.
- ✓ We can import multiple modules with a single import statement, but a module is loaded once regardless of the number of times, it has been imported into our file.
- ✓ The syntax to use the import statement is given below.

Syntax-1 **import module_name**
Syntax-2 **import module1,module2,........ module n**

Note: When we are using a function from a module, then we use the following syntax to access the module:

```
Syntax
module_name.function_name
```

- ✓ Hence, if we need to call the function ***display()*** defined in the file ***eee.py***, we have to import that file as a module into our new python program as shown in the example:

Example

```
import cse
name = input("Enter the name:")
cse.display(name)
```

Output

```
Enter the name: Priya
Hi Priya
```

ii.The from-import statement:

- ✓ Instead of importing the whole module into the namespace, python provides the flexibility to import only the specific attributes of a module.
- ✓ This can be done by using ***"from-import"*** statement.
- ✓ The syntax to use the "***from-import"*** statement is:

Syntax-1 **from** module-name **import** function_name
Syntax-2 **from** module-name **import** function 1 , function 2.., function n

- ✓ Consider the following module named as eee which contains three functions as sum, mul and div

eee.py

```
def sum(a,b):
   return a+b
def mul(a,b):
   return a*b;
def div(a,b):
   return a/b;
```

Main.py

```
from cse import sum
a = int(input("Enter the first number"))
b = int(input("Enter the second number"))
print("Result is: ",sum(a,b))
```

NOTE: Here we have to note that when we try to import using the from keyword, then do not use the module name when referring to elements in the module.

2.3 Variables in Python Modules:

- ✓ The module can contain functions, as already described, but can also contain variables of all types such as arrays, dictionaries, objects, etc.

```
EEE.py

d = {"name": "Ram", "age": 26,"country": "India"}
```

- ✓ Import the module named mymodule, and access the person1 dictionary:

```
import CSE
a = CSE.d["age"]
print(a)
```

2.4 How to rename a Python Module:

- ✓ We can name the file of the module whatever you like, but we have to note that it must have the file extension ".py".
- ✓ To rename the module name, we can create an alias when you import a module, with the help of the "**as**" keyword.
- ✓ The syntax to rename a module is :

```
Syntax
import module_name as new_name
```

```
cse.py
def sum(a,b):
    return a+b
```

```
Main.py
import cse as c
a = int(input("Enter the first number"))
```

```
b = int(input("Enter the second number"))
res=c.sum(a,b)
print("Result is: ",res)
```

2.5 Advantages of Modules:

i. **Reusability:** Working with modules makes the code reusable.

ii. **Simplicity:** The module focuses on a small proportion of the problem, rather than focusing on the entire problem.

iii. **Scoping:** A separate namespace is defined by a module that helps to avoid collisions between identifiers.

2.6. Python Built-in Modules:

- ✓ As we know that the Python interactive shell has a number of built- in functions.
- ✓ As a shell start, these functions are loaded automatically and are always available, such as,print() and input() for I/O,Number conversion functions such as int(), float(), complex(),Data type conversions such as list(), tuple(), set(), etc.
- ✓ In addition to these many built-in functions, there are also a large number of pre-defined functions available as a part of libraries bundled with Python distributions.
- ✓ These functions are defined in modules which are known as built-in modules.
- ✓ These built-in modules are written in C language and integrated with the Python shell.
- ✓ To display a list of all of the available modules in Python Programming Language, we can use the following command in the Python console:
- ✓ **help('modules')**
- ✓ Built-in modules of Python
    - i. Math Module
    - ii. Statistics Module

i. Math Module of Python:

- ✓ Most popular mathematical functions that are defined in the math module include,
    - → Trigonometric functions
    - → Representation functions
    - → Logarithmic functions
    - → Angle conversion functions, etc.

- ✓ In addition, two mathematical constants- pi and e are also defined in this module.
- ✓ In Mathematics, Pi is a well-known mathematical constant. Its value is 3.141592653589793.

```
>>> import math
>>>math.pi
3.141592653589793
```

- ✓ In this example, we will find the value of sin, cos, and tan ratios for the angle of 30 degrees which in radians is equal to 0.5235987755982988 radians.

```
>>> import math
>>>math.sin(0.5235987755982988)
        0.49999999999999994
>>>math.cos(0.5235987755982988)
        0.8660254037844387
>>>math.tan(0.5235987755982988)
        0.5773502691896257
```

- ✓ Many more functions of the math module such as math.log(),
- ✓ math.log10() math.pow() math.sqrt() math.exp() math.ceil() math.floor() etc.

2.7 Working with Statistics Module of Python:

- ✓ The statistics module provides functions to mathematical statistics of numeric data. Some of the popular statistical functions are defined in this module are as follows:
    i. Mean
    ii. Median
    iii. Mode
    iv. Standard Deviation

i. Mean:

- ✓ The mean() method returns the arithmetic mean of the numbers present in a list.

```
>>> import statistics
>>>statistics.mean([3,4,7,8])
    5.5
```

ii. Median:

- ✓ The median() method returns the middle value of numeric data present in a list.

```
>>> import statistics
>>>statistics.median([1,2,3,7,8,9])
    5.0
>>>statistics.median([1,2,3,8,9])
    3.0
```

iii. Mode:

- ✓ The mode() method returns the most common data point present in the list.

```
>>> import statistics
>>>statistics.mode([2,5,3,2,8,3,9,4,2,5,6])
    2
```

iv. Standard Deviation:

- ✓ The stdev() method returns the standard deviation on a given sample in the form of a list.

For Example,

```
>>> import statistics
>>>statistics.stdev ([1,1.5,2,2.5,3,3.5,4,4.5,5])
    1.3693063937629153
```

Ex: Write a python program to define a module to find Fibonacci Numbers and import the module to another program

```
ram.py
# Fibonacci numbers module
def fib(n):
    a, b = 0, 1
    while b < n:
        print(b, end=' ')
        a, b = b, a+b
```

```
sai.py
import ram
n=int(input("Enter n value:"))
ram.fib(n)
```

Ex: Write a python program to define a module and import aspecific function in that module to another program.

```
cse.py
def sum(a,b):
  return a+b
def mul(a,b):
  return a*b;
def div(a,b):
  return a/b;
```

```
Main.py
from cse import sum
a = int(input("Enter the first number"))
b = int(input("Enter the second number"))
print("Result is: ",sum(a,b))
```

3.Packages:

- ✓ We organize a large number of files in different folders and subfolders based on some criteria, so that we can find and manage them easily.
- ✓ In the same way, a package in Python takes the concept of the modular approach to next logical level.
- ✓ As you know, a module can contain multiple objects, such as classes, functions, etc.
- ✓ A package can contain one or more relevant modules.
- ✓ Physically, a package is actually a folder containing one or more module files.
- ✓ A package is basically a directory with Python files and a file with the name __init__.py.
- ✓ It's possible to put several modules into a Package.

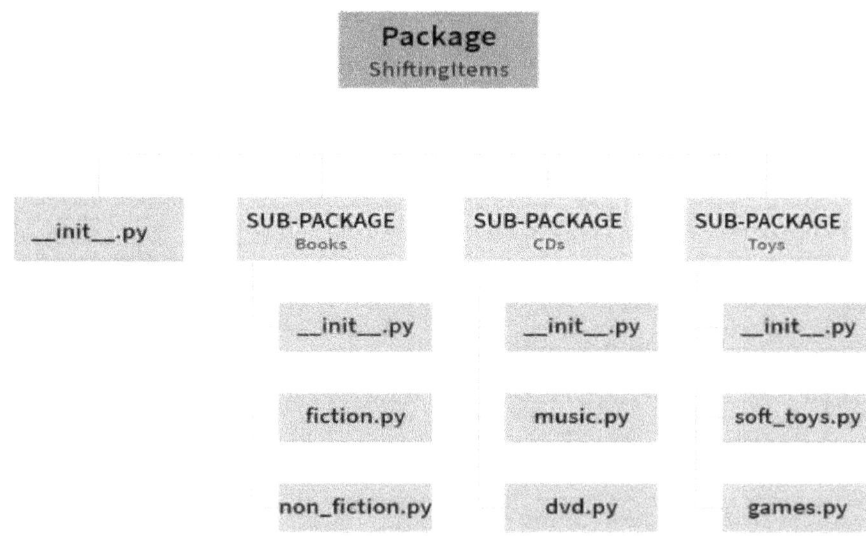

- ✓ Let's create a package named mypackage, using the following steps:
  - i. Create a new folder named D:\MyApp.
  - ii. Inside MyApp, create a subfolder with the name 'mypackage'.
  - iii. Create an empty __init__.py file in the mypackage folder.
  - iv. Using a Python-aware editor like IDLE, create modules **greet.py** and **functions.py** with the following code:

```
greet.py
def SayHello(name):
        print("Hello ", name)
```

```
functions.py
def sum(x,y):
        return x+y
def average(x,y):
        return (x+y)/2
def power(x,y):
        return x**y
```

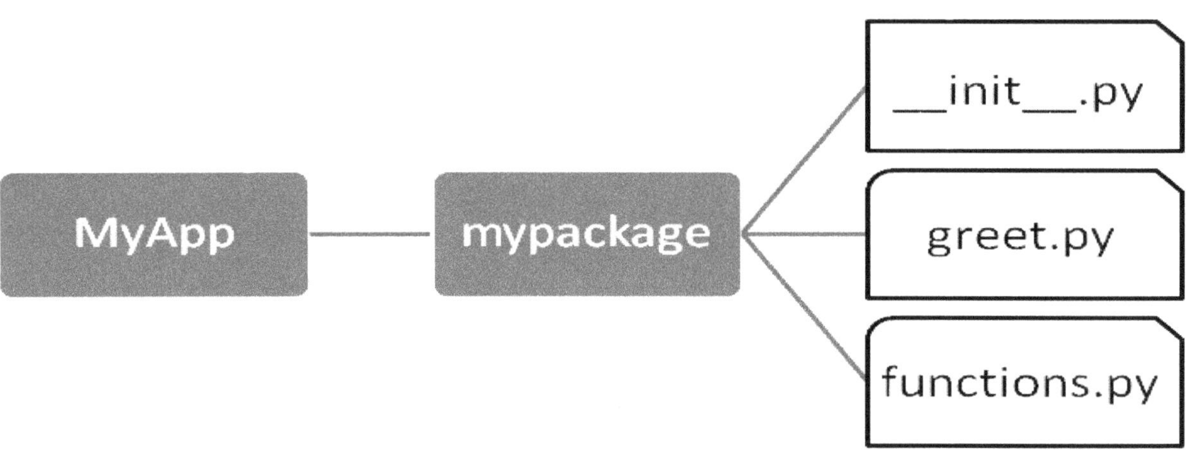

3.1 Importing module from a package:

- ✓ We can import modules from packages using the dot (.) operator.
- ✓ Import the ***functions module*** from the ***mypackage*** and **call** its ***power() function.***

```
>>>from mypackage import functions
>>>functions.power(3,2)
 9
```

```
def check():
    a=int(input('Enter a number'))
    if a%2==0:
print("Even")
    else:
        print("Odd")
```

```
>>> import check as check
>>> check()
```

5. Classes in Python

- ✓ **1. Principles of object orientation:**
  - i. Classes
  - ii. Objects
  - iii. Abstraction
  - iv. Encapsulation
  - v. Inheritance
  - vi. Polymorphism

- ❖ **Class:** OOP in Python is class-based and your objects will be defined with the class keyword
- ❖ **Object:** Objects purposely represent real-world objects or things like a car or flower. Python objects have a collection of related properties or behaviors like model() or colour().
- ❖ **Abstraction:**Abstraction is the concept of hiding all the implementation of your class away from anything outside of the class.
- ❖ **Encapsulation:**Encapsulation is the method of keeping all the state, variables, and methods private unless declared to be public.
- ❖ **Inheritance:**Inheritance is the mechanism for creating a child class thatcaninheritbehaviorandpropertiesfromaparent(derived)class.
- ❖ **Polymorphism:**Polymorphism is a way of interfacing with objects and receiving different forms or results.

2.Creating Class:

- ✓ A class is a collection of objects or you can say it is a blueprint of objects defining the common attributes and behavior.
- ✓ A class is a virtual entity and can be seen as a blueprint of an object. The class came into existence when it instantiated.
- ✓ A class contains the properties (attribute) and action (behavior) of the object. Properties represent variables, and the methods represent actions. Hence class includes both variables and methods.
- ✓ On the other hand, the object is the instance of a class. The process of creating an object can be called instantiation.
- ✓ As class is collection of attributes and methods.

Example:

- ✓ Suppose a class is a prototype of a building. A building contains all the details about the floor, rooms, doors, windows, etc. we can make as many buildings as we want, based on these details. Hence, the building can be seen as a class, and we can create as many objects of this class.
- ✓ In Python, a class can be created by using the keyword class, followed by the class name. The syntax to create a class is given below.
- ✓ Attributes are the variables that belong to a class.
- ✓ Attributes are always public and can be accessed using the dot (.) operator.
- ✓ The Class is defined under a "Class" Keyword
- ✓ The syntax of the Class Definition is:

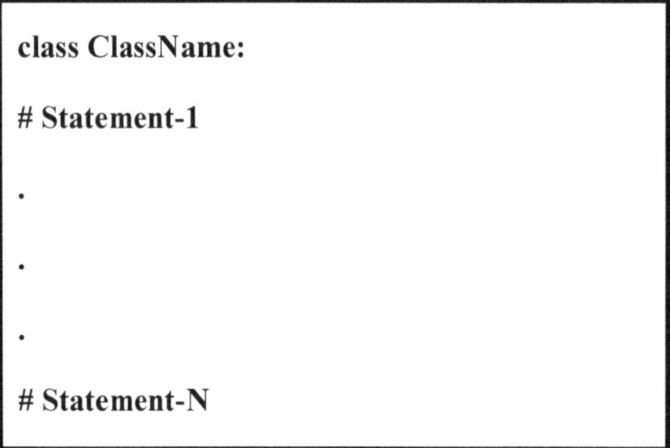

```
class ClassName:
# Statement-1
.
.
.
# Statement-N
```

Example	**Example**

class MyClass:
    x =5
	class Book:
	def details(self):
	    print("This is python Book")

2.1 The pass Statement:

- ✓ class definitions cannot be empty, but for some reason if you have a class definition with no content, put in the pass statement to avoid getting an error.

```
Example
class Person:
    pass
```

3. Creating Object:

- ✓ When an object of a class is created, the class is said to be instantiated.
- ✓ All the instances share the attributes and the behavior of the class.
- ✓ A single class may have any number of instances.
- ✓ A class needs to be instantiated if we want to use the class attributes in another class or method.
- ✓ A class can be instantiated by calling the class using the class name.
- ✓ The class object could be used to access different attributes.
- ✓ Attributes may be data or method. Methods of an object are corresponding functions of that class.
- ✓ The syntax to create the instance of the class is given below:
- ✓

```
Syntax
object-name = class-name(arguments)
```

```
Example
class MyClass:
    x =5
p1=MyClass()
print(p1.x)
p1.fun()
```

4. Constructor in Python:

The _init_( ) method:

- ✓ The __init()__ method is called the constructor in Python.
- ✓ It is a special method that starts and ends with two underscores and is invoked or calls automatically when object is created for class.
- ✓ Constructor is a special method used to create and initialize an object of a class.
- ✓ Like methods, a constructor also contains a collection of statements that are executed at the time of Object creation.
- ✓ It runs as soon as an object of a class is instantiated. The method is useful to do any initialization you want to do with your object.
- ✓ All classes have a function called __init__(), which is always executed when the class is being initiated.

Syntax

```
def __init__(self):
   # body of the constructor
```

Here,

→ *def:* The keyword is used to define function.

→ *__init__() :* It is a reserved method. This method gets called as soon as an object of a class is instantiated.

→ *self:* The first argument self refers to the current object. It binds the instance to the __init__() method. It's usually named self to follow the naming convention.

Example

```
class Person:
def __init__(self, name, age):
self.name = name
```

```
self.age = age
p1 = Person("John", 36)
print(p1.name)
print(p1.age)
```

```
class employee():
def __init__(self,name,age,salary):
    self.name = name
self.age = age
self.salary = salary
emp1 = employee("Hemanth",22,1234)
emp2 = employee("Sai",23, 2234)
```

```
class Book:
def __init__(self, title,  author, price):
self.title = title
self.author = author
self.price = price
b1 = Book('Python', 'abc', 120)
b2 = Book('Java', 'xyz', 220)
print(b1)
print(b2)
```

```
Output:
<__main__.Book object at 0x00000156EE59A9D0>
<__main__.Book object at 0x00000156EE59A8B0>
```

- ✓ b1, b2 are distinct objects of the class Book. The term self in the attributes refers to the corresponding instances (objects).
- ✓ The class and memory location of the objects are printed when they are printed.
- ✓ We can't expect them to provide specific information such as the title, author name, and so on.
- ✓ But we can use a specific method called __repr__ to do this.
- ✓ In Python, a special method is a defined function that starts and ends with two underscores and is invoked automatically when certain conditions are met.

```
class Book:
def __init__(self, title, author, price):
self.title = title
self.author = author
self.price = price

def __repr__(self):
return f"Book: {self.title}, Author: {self.author}, Price:{self.price}"

b1 = Book('Python', 'abc', 120)
b2 = Book('Java', 'xyz', 220)
print(b1)
print(b2)
```

Output

Book: Python, Author: abc, Price: 120

Book: Java, Author: xyz, Price: 220

5. The self-parameter:

- ✓ The self-parameter refers to the current instance or current object of the class and accesses the class variables.
- ✓ We can use anything instead of self, but it must be the first parameter of any function which belongs to the class.
- ✓ Class methods must have an extra first parameter in the method definition. We do not give a value for this parameter when we call the method, Python provides it.
- ✓ If we have a method that takes no arguments, then we still have to have one argument i.e. self.

6. Instance Variables & class variables:

- ✓ Python class variables are declared within a class and their values are the same across all instances of a class.
- ✓ Python instance variables can have different values across multiple instances of a class.
- ✓ Class variables share the same value among all instances of the class. The value of instance variables can differ across each instance of a class.
- ✓ Instance variables are for data, unique to each instance and class variables are for attributes and methods shared by all instances of the class.
- ✓ Instance variables are variables whose value is assigned inside a constructor or method with "self" whereas class variables are variables whose value is assigned in the class.
- ✓ class variables are variables whose value is assigned in the class.

class variables Example	**Instance Variables Example**
class Shark:	class Shark:
name = "fish"	def __init__(self, name):

obj = Shark() print(obj.name)	self.name = name obj1 = Shark("Sammy") print(obj1.name) obj2 = Shark("Stevie") print(obj2.name)
Output **Fish**	**Output** Sammy Stevie

7. Python Inheritance:

- ✓ In inheritance, the child class acquires the properties and can access all the data members and functions defined in the parent class.
- ✓ A child class can also provide its specific implementation to the functions of the parent class.
- ✓ Inheritance is the ability to 'inherit' features or attributes from already written classes into newer classes we make.
- ✓
- ✓ Inheritance provides code reusability to the program because we can use an existing class to create a new class instead of creating it from scratch.

i.Single Inheritance:

- ✓ Single Inheritance is the simplest form of inheritance where a single child class or derived class is derived from a single parent class.

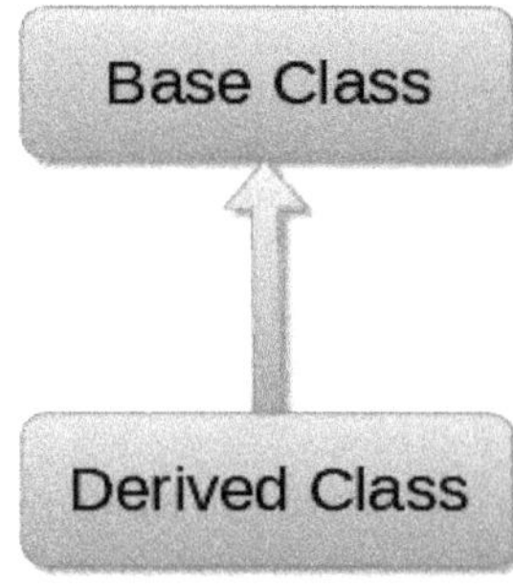

Syntax

class derived_class_name(base class):

<class-suite>

✓ A class can inherit multiple classes by mentioning all of them inside the bracket. Consider the following syntax.

Syntax

class derive-class(<base class 1>, <base class 2>, .. <base class n>):

<class - suite>

Example	**Output**

class Animal:
def speak(self):
print("Animal Speaking")
class Dog(Animal):
def bark(self):
print("dog barking")
d = Dog()
d.bark()
d.speak()
	dog barking
	Animal Speaking

# Create Base class 	
class Vehicle:
 	
def __init__(self, name, color, price):
self.name = name
self.color = color
self.price = price
	Output
	BMW X1 Black 35000
	BMW X1 5

def info(self):
print(self.name, self.color, self.price)
 	
# Create a Child class 	
class Car(Vehicle):
defchange_gear(self, no):
print(self.name, no)
 	
# Create object for Car 	
obj = Car('BMW X1', 'Black', 35000)
obj.info()
obj.change_gear(5)	

ii. Multi-Level inheritance:

- ✓ Multi-level inheritance is archived when a derived class inherits another derived class.
- ✓ There is no limit on the number of levels up to which, the multi-level inheritance is archived in python.
- ✓ The syntax of multi-level inheritance is:

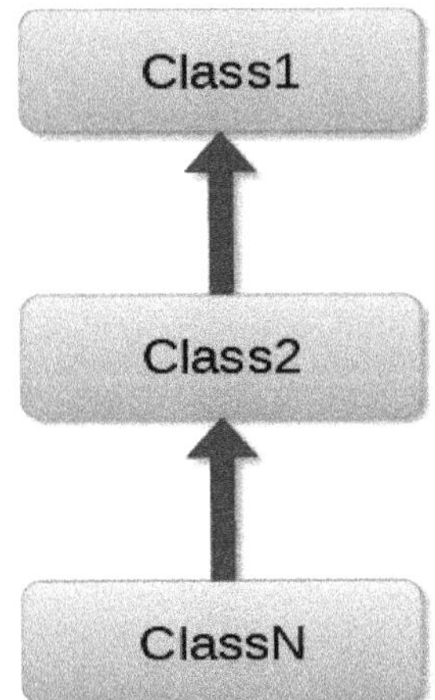

Syntax

```
class class1:
 <class-suite>
class class2(class1):
 <class suite>
class class3(class2):
        <class suite>
```

Example	**Output**

class Animal:
 def speak(self):
  print("Animal Speaking")
class Dog(Animal):
def bark(self):
  print("dog barking")
class DogChild(Dog):
def eat(self):
  print("Eating bread...")
d =DogChild()
d.bark()
d.speak()
d.eat()
	dog barking
	Animal Speaking
	Eating bread...

Example
 	
class parent1:
def func1:
print("Hello Parent1")
class parent2
def func2:
print("Hello Parent2")
class child(parent1, parent2):
def func3:
print("Hello Child")
t=child()
t.func1()
t.func2()
t.func3()
	Output
	Hello Parent1
	Hello Parent2
	Hello Child

iii.Multiple inheritance:

- ✓ Python provides us the flexibility to inherit multiple base classes in the child class.

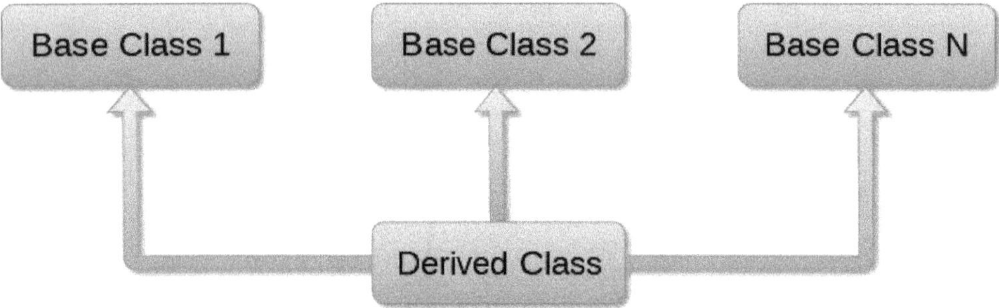

✓ The syntax to perform multiple inheritance is:

Syntax
```
class Base1:
<class-suite>

class Base2:
<class-suite>
.
.
.
class BaseN:
<class-suite>

classDerived_class_name(Base1, Base2, ...... BaseN):
<class-suite>
```

Example	**Output**

class Cal_1:
def Sum(self,a,b):
    return a+b
class Cal_2:
defMul(self,a,b):
   return a*b
class Derived(Cal_1,Cal_2):
defDiv(self,a,b):
    return a/b
d = Derived()
print(d.Sum(10,20))
	30
	200
	0.5

print(d.Mul(10,20)) print(d.Div(10,20))	

Advantages of Inheritance in Python:

i. **Modular Codebase:** Increases modularity i.e. breaking down codebase into modules which makes it easier to understand. Here, each class that we define becomes a separate module that can be separately inherited by one or many classes.

ii. **Code Reusability**: the child class copies all the attributes and methods of the parent class into its own class and use. This saves time and coding effort by not rewriting them thus following modularity paradigms.

iii. **Less Development**: and Maintenance Costs: changes just need to be made in the base class, all derived classes will automatically follow.

Disadvantages of Inheritance in Python:

i. **Decreases the Execution Speed**: loading multiple classes because they are interdependent on each other

ii. **Tightly Coupled Classes**: this means that even though parent classes can be executed independently, child classes cannot be executed without defining their parent classes.

1. Introduction to Regular Expression:

- ✓ A Regular Expressionis a sequence of characters that forms a search pattern.
- ✓ RegEx can be used to check if a string contains the specified search pattern.
- ✓ A regular expression is a set of characters with highly specialized syntax that we can use to find or match other characters or groups of characters.
- ✓ In short, regular expressions, or Regex, are widely used in the UNIX world.
- ✓ For example,

Example

^a...s$

- ✓ The above code defines a RegEx pattern. The pattern is: **any five letter string starting with a and ending with s**.
- ✓ A pattern defined using RegEx can be used to match against a string.

Expression	String	Matched?
^a...s$	abs	No match
	alias	Match
	abyss	Match
	Alias	No match
	An abacus	No match

- ✓ The re-module in Python gives full support for regular expressions.
- ✓ The re module raises the re.error exception whenever an error occurs while implementing or using a regular expression.
- ✓ Python has a built-in package called re, which can be used to work with Regular Expressions.
- ✓ Import the re module:

Syntax

```
import re
```

2. MetaCharacters:

- ✓ Metacharacters are characters that are interpreted in a special way by a RegEx engine. Here's a list of metacharacters:

[] . ^ $ * + ? {} () \ |

i. Square brackets([ ]):

- ✓ Square brackets specifies a set of characters you wish to match.

Expression	String	Matched?
[abc]	a	1 match
	ac	2 matches
	Hey Jude	No match

	abc de ca	5 matches

- ✓ Here, [abc] will match if the string you are trying to match contains any of the a, b or c.
- ✓ You can also specify a range of characters using - inside square brackets.
- ✓ [a-e] is the same as [abcde].
- ✓ [1-4] is the same as [1234].
- ✓ [0-39] is the same as [01239].
- ✓ You can complement (invert) the character set by using caret ^ symbol at the start of a square-bracket.
- ✓ [^abc] means any character except a or b or c.
- ✓ [^0-9] means any non-digit character.

ii . Period (..):

- ✓ A period matches any single character (except newline '\n').

Expression	String	Matched?
..	a	No match
	ac	1 match
	acd	1 match
	acde	2 matches (contains 4 characters)

iii. Caret(^):

- ✓ The caret symbol ^ is used to check if a string **starts with** a certain character.

Expression	String	Matched?
^a	a	1 match
	abc	1 match
	bac	No match
^ab	abc	1 match
	acb	No match (starts with a but not followed by b)

iv. Dollar($):

- ✓ The dollar symbol $ is used to check if a string **ends with** a certain character.

Expression	String	Matched?
a$	a	1 match
	formula	1 match
	cab	No match

v. Star(*):

✓ The star symbol * matches **zero or more occurrences** of the pattern left to it.

Expression	String	Matched?
ma*n	mn	1 match
	man	1 match
	maaan	1 match
	main	No match (a is not followed by n)
	woman	1 match

vi. Plus(+):

✓ The plus symbol + matches **one or more occurrences** of the pattern left to it.

Expression	String	Matched?
ma+n	mn	No match (no a character)
	man	1 match
	maaan	1 match
	main	No match (a is not followed by n)
	woman	1 match

vii.Question Mark(?):

The question mark symbol ? matches **zero or one occurrence** of the pattern left to it.

Expression	String	Matched?
ma?n	mn	1 match
	man	1 match
	maaan	No match (more than one a character)
	main	No match (a is not followed by n)
	woman	1 match

vii. Braces({ }):

✓ Consider this code: {n,m}. This means at least n, and at most m repetitions of the pattern left to it.

Expression	String	Matched?
a{2,3}	abcdat	No match
	abcdaat	1 match (at daat)
	aabcdaaat	2 matches (at aabc and daaat)
	aabcdaaaat	2 matches (at aabc and daaaat)

✓ Let's try one more example. This RegEx [0-9]{2, 4} matches at least 2 digits but not more than 4 digits

Expression	String	Matched?
[0-9]{2,4}	ab123csde	1 match (match at ab123csde)

	12 and 345673	3 matches (12, 3456, 73)
	1 and 2	No match

ix . Alternation(|):

- ✓ Vertical bar | is used for alternation (or operator).

Expression	String	Matched?
a|b	cde	No match
	ade	1 match (match at ade)
	acdbea	3 matches (at acdbea)

- ✓ Here, a|b match any string that contains either a or b

x. Group ( ):

- ✓ Parentheses () is used to group sub-patterns. For example, (a|b|c)xz match any string that matches either a or b or c followed by xz

Expression	String	Matched?
(a|b|c)xz	ab xz	No match
	abxz	1 match (match at abxz)
	axzcabxz	2 matches (at axzbccabxz)

xi. Backslash(\):

- ✓ Backlash \ is used to escape various characters including all metacharacters. For example,
- ✓ \$a match if a string contains $ followed by a. Here, $ is not interpreted by a RegEx engine in a special way.
- ✓ If you are unsure if a character has special meaning or not, you can put \ in front of it. This makes sure the character is not treated in a special way.

3.Special Sequences:

- ✓ Special sequences make commonly used patterns easier to write. Here's a list of special sequences:
- ✓ \A - Matches if the specified characters are at the start of a string.

Expression	String	Matched?
\Athe	the sun	Match
	In the sun	No match

- ✓ \b - Matches if the specified characters are at the beginning or end of a word.

Expression	String	Matched?
\bfoo	football	Match
	a football	Match
	afootball	No match
foo\b	the foo	Match
	the afoo test	Match
	the afootest	No match

✓ \B - Opposite of \b. matches if the specified characters are **not** at the beginning or end of a word.

Expression	String	Matched?
\Bfoo	football	No match
	a football	No match
	afootball	Match
foo\B	the foo	No match
	the afoo test	No match
	the afootest	Match

✓ \d - Matches any decimal digit. Equivalent to [0-9]

Expression	String	Matched?
\d	12abc3	3 matches (at 12abc3)
	Python	No match

✓ \D - Matches any non-decimal digit. Equivalent to [^0-9]

Expression	String	Matched?
\D	1ab34"50	3 matches (at 1ab34"50)
	1345	No match

✓ \s - Matches where a string contains any whitespace character. Equivalent to [\t\n\r\f\v].

Expression	String	Matched?
\s	Python RegEx	1 match
	PythonRegEx	No match

✓ \S - Matches where a string contains any non-whitespace character. Equivalent to [^ \t\n\r\f\v].

Expression	String	Matched?
\S	a b	2 matches (at ab)
		No match

✓ \w - Matches any alphanumeric character (digits and alphabets). Equivalent to [a-zA-Z0-9_]. By the way, underscore _ is also considered an alphanumeric character.

Expression	String	Matched?
\w	12&": ;c	3 matches (at 12&": ;c)
	%"> !	No match

✓ \W - Matches any non-alphanumeric character. Equivalent to [^a-zA-Z0-9_]

Expression	String	Matched?
\W	1a2%c	1 match (at 1a2%c)
	Python	No match

- ✓ \Z - Matches if the specified characters are at the end of a string.

Expression	String	Matched?
Python\Z	I like Python	1 match
	I like Python Programming	No match
	Python is fun.	No match

Metacharacters:

<table>
<tr><th>Character</th><th>Description</th><th>Example</th></tr>
<tr><td>[]</td><td>A set of characters</td><td>"[a-m]"</td></tr>
<tr><td>\</td><td>Signals a special sequence (can also be used to escape special characters)</td><td>"\d"</td></tr>
<tr><td>.</td><td>Any character (except newline character)</td><td>"he..o"</td></tr>
<tr><td>^</td><td>Starts with</td><td>"^hello"</td></tr>
<tr><td>$</td><td>Ends with</td><td>"planet$"</td></tr>
<tr><td>*</td><td>Zero or more occurrences</td><td>"he.*o"</td></tr>
<tr><td>+</td><td>One or more occurrences</td><td>"he.+o"</td></tr>
<tr><td>?</td><td>Zero or one occurrences</td><td>"he.?o"</td></tr>
<tr><td>{}</td><td>Exactly the specified number of occurrences</td><td>"he.{2}o"</td></tr>
<tr><td>|</td><td>Either or</td><td>"falls|stays"</td></tr>
<tr><td>()</td><td>Capture and group</td><td></td></tr>
</table>

Special Sequences:

- ✓ A special sequence is a \ followed by one of the characters in the list below, and has a special meaning:

Character	Description	Example
\A	Returns a match if the specified characters are at the beginning of the string	"\AThe"
\b	Returns a match where the specified characters are at the beginning or at the end of a word (the "r" in the beginning is making sure that the string is being treated as a "raw string")	r"\bain" r"ain\b"

\B	Returns a match where the specified characters are present, but NOT at the beginning (or at the end) of a word (the "r" in the beginning is making sure that the string is being treated as a "raw string")	r"\Bain" r"ain\B"
\d	Returns a match where the string contains digits (numbers from 0-9)	"\d"
\D	Returns a match where the string DOES NOT contain digits	"\D"
\s	Returns a match where the string contains a white space character	"\s"
\S	Returns a match where the string DOES NOT contain a white space character	"\S"
\w	Returns a match where the string contains any word characters (characters from a to Z, digits from 0-9, and the underscore _ character)	"\w"
\W	Returns a match where the string DOES NOT contain any word characters	"\W"
\Z	Returns a match if the specified characters are at the end of the string	"Spain\Z"

4. RegEx Functions:

- ✓ The re module offers a set of functions that allows us to search a string for a match:

Function	Description
findall	Returns a list containing all matches
search	Returns a Match object if there is a match anywhere in the string
split	Returns a list where the string has been split at each match
sub	Replaces one or many matches with a string

i.findall() Function

- ✓ The findall() function returns a list containing all matches.

Example-1

#Print a list of all matches:

```
import re
txt = "The rain in Spain"
x = re.findall("ai", txt)
print(x)
```

Example-2

 # Program to extract numbers from a string

```
import re
string = 'hello 12 hi 89. Howdy 34'
pattern = '\d+'
result = re.findall(pattern, string)
print(result)

# Output: ['12', '89', '34']
```

- ✓ The list contains the matches in the order they are found.
- ✓ If no matches are found, an empty list is returned

ii.search() Function:

- ✓ The search() function searches the string for a match, and returns a Match object if there is a match.
- ✓ If there is more than one match, only the first occurrence of the match will be returned.
- ✓ The re.search() method takes two arguments: a pattern and a string. The method looks for the first location where the RegEx pattern produces a match with the string.
- ✓ If the search is successful, re.search() returns a match object; if not, it returns None
- ✓ Syntax is:**match = re.search(pattern, str)**

Example-1

#Search for the first white-space character in the string

```
import re
txt = "The rain in Spain"
x = re.search("\s", txt)
```

```
print("The first white-space character is located in position:", x.start())
```

Example-2

```
import re
string = "Python is fun"

# check if 'Python' is at the beginning
match = re.search('\APython', string)

if match:
  print("pattern found inside the string")
else:
  print("pattern not found")
```

Output: pattern found inside the string

iii.split() Function

- ✓ The split() function returns a list where the string has been split at each match:

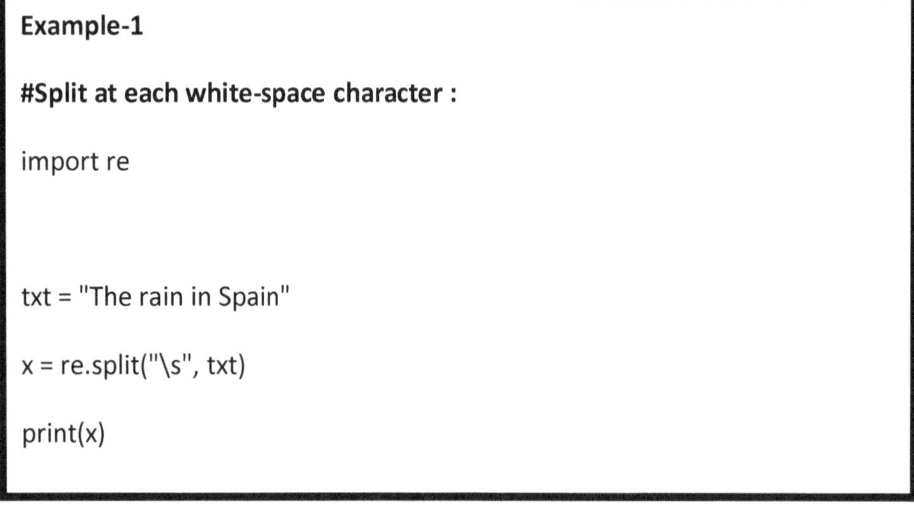

Example-1

#Split at each white-space character :

```
import re

txt = "The rain in Spain"
x = re.split("\s", txt)
print(x)
```

Example-2

```
import re

string = 'Twelve:12 Eighty nine:89.'

pattern = '\d+'

result = re.split(pattern, string)

print(result)
```

Output: ['Twelve:', ' Eighty nine:', '.']

iv.sub() Function:

- ✓ The sub() function replaces the matches with the text of your choice
- ✓ The syntax of re.sub() is:

re.sub(pattern, replace, string)

- ✓ The method returns a string where matched occurrences are replaced with the content of replace variable.

Example-1

#Replace every white-space character with the number 9:

```
import re

txt = "The rain in Spain"

x = re.sub("\s", "9", txt)

print(x)
```

Example-2

 # Program to remove all whitespaces

```
import re

string = 'abc 12\

de 23 \n f45 6'

pattern = '\s+'

replace = ''
```

```
new_string = re.sub(pattern, replace, string)

print(new_string)
```

Output: abc12de23f456

Match Object

- ✓ A Match Object is an object containing information about the search and the result.
- ✓ You can get methods and attributes of a match object using dir() function.
- ✓ Some of the commonly used methods and attributes of match objects are:

Note: If there is no match, the value None will be returned, instead of the Match Object.

Example

#Do a search that will return a Match Object :

```
import re

txt = "The rain in Spain"

x = re.search("ai", txt)

print(x)
```

- ✓ The Match object has properties and methods used to retrieve information about the search, and the result:

i.span()

- ✓ It returns a tuple containing the start-, and end positions of the match.

Example

#The regular expression looks for any words that starts with an upper case "S"::

```
import re

txt = "The rain in Spain"

x = re.search(r"\bS\w+", txt)
```

```
print(x.span())
```

ii.string:

- ✓ It returns the string passed into the function

Example

#Print the string passed into the function

```
import re

txt = "The rain in Spain"

x = re.search(r"\bS\w+", txt)

print(x.string)
```

iii.group():

- ✓ It returns the part of the string where there was a match

Example-1

#Print the string passed into the function

```
import re

txt = "The rain in Spain"

x = re.search(r"\bS\w+", txt)

print(x.group())
```

Example-2

```
import re
```

```
string = '39801 356, 2102 1111'

pattern = '(\d{3}) (\d{2})'

match = re.search(pattern, string)

if match:

  print(match.group())

else:

  print("pattern not found")
```

Output: 801 35

match.start(), match.end()

- ✓ The start() function returns the index of the start of the matched substring. Similarly, end() returns the end index of the matched substring.

Example

```
>>>match.start()

2

>>>match.end()

8
```

Epilogue

Congratulations on completing *Zero to Python: A Beginner's Coding Pathway*! You've journeyed from your first steps in programming to mastering the foundational concepts of Python. Along the way, you've developed not only coding skills but also the confidence to tackle new challenges.

This book was designed to be your introduction to the world of programming, and I hope it has inspired you to continue exploring the endless possibilities that Python and other programming languages offer. Whether you plan to build applications, analyze data, or create something entirely new, you now have the tools to begin making your ideas a reality.

But remember, learning to code is a lifelong journey. The concepts you've learned here are just the beginning. The world of technology is always evolving, and with your new skills, you're well-equipped to keep up with those changes and grow as a programmer.

As you move forward, don't be afraid to experiment, make mistakes, and learn from them. The beauty of programming is that every challenge is an opportunity to improve and innovate. Continue to build on what you've learned, seek out new knowledge, and most importantly, keep coding.

Thank you for choosing *Zero to Python* as your guide on this journey. I wish you all the best in your future coding adventures. The world is full of possibilities—go out and create something amazing!

www.ingramcontent.com/pod-product-compliance
Lightning Source LLC
LaVergne TN
LVHW070934160826
845679LV00021B/1803
9798896100447